A New History of Wales

A New History of Wales

Myths and Realities in Welsh History

Edited by

H.V. Bowen

Gomer

Published in 2011 by
Gomer Press, Llandysul, Ceredigion, SA44 4JL

ISBN 978 1 84851 373 0

A CIP record for this title is available from the British Library.

This book is published with the financial support of the
Welsh Books Council.

Printed and bound in Wales at
Gomer Press, Llandysul, Ceredigion

Acknowledgements

I would like to thank the Editor of the *Western Mail*, Alan Edmunds, for inviting History Research Wales to collaborate in the exciting project that created the 24 newspaper feature articles that now form the substance of this book. It has been a pleasure working with Alan and his colleagues, and I say that as an academic who is used to operating at a pace that is a little slower than that of a journalist. I am especially indebted to Ceri-Gould Thomas, Executive Editor Media Wales, who offered calm, reassuring advice throughout, and then managed the production of the newspaper articles in exemplary fashion. Tony Woolway, the Chief Librarian of Media Wales, was immensely helpful when it came to the selection of many of the images to be found in this book. I thank Russell Deacon of UWIC who was instrumental in bringing History Research Wales and the *Western Mail* together in the first place; and Ceri Wyn Jones of Gomer Press for all his work in making this book possible. Most of all, though, I offer my thanks to the authors of the essays. It would have been easy for them to duck the challenge, not least because they are extremely busy men and women who are often carrying very heavy teaching and administrative loads at a time of great uncertainty in British universities. But they all responded to the call with enormous enthusiasm, and to my great astonishment (and I suspect to the astonishment of many at the *Western Mail*) they actually delivered their essays on time. *Diolch yn fawr*!

Contents

Contents (*continued*)

Introduction

H.V. Bowen

In many ways this is a highly unusual book. It is unusual because it represents the outcome of a unique collaboration between a daily national newspaper, the *Western Mail*, and a group of twenty academic historians who form part of History Research Wales. HRW is collaborative research partnership established in 2009 between the Departments or Schools of History and Archaeology and/ or Welsh History in the Welsh universities. A key part of HRW's mission is to ensure that the very latest research findings in history (and not just Welsh history) are made available to public audiences in Wales, the UK, and the wider world.

It is fair to say, I think, that journalists and academics have traditionally had a somewhat uneasy relationship. Many academics have tended to be rather sniffy about the Fourth Estate, regarding its denizens as untrustworthy, whisky-fuelled, intellectual lightweights who are in the business of producing today's cheap quote and tomorrow's fish and chip wrappers. Indeed, I suspect that a few of my colleagues still think this! On the other hand, journalists have often regarded academics – and especially professors – as feckless, gin-soaked wasters who are out of touch with the 'real world'. Living off the taxpayer, their bodies are in the Ivory Tower, their heads in the clouds, and their wandering thoughts in places that one can only speculate (and worry) about. They write books on arcane subjects that interest no one other than fellow oddballs.

But in case the reader is already worried about the state of our livers and minds, I am happy to report that the close collaborative work that went into the making of this book has, if nothing else, already served finally to destroy these lazy and outdated stereotypes. This is quite appropriate in view of the fact that this volume is dedicated to exploring and exploding some of the many myths and popular misunderstandings that abound in Welsh history.

The essays that follow were first published in the *Western Mail* in September and October 2010. Over the course of four weeks, the newspaper published a daily essay of 2,500 words, each written by one of my colleagues, each of whom had been given free rein to write about how their latest research threw new light on the history of Wales. I stand to be corrected, but I cannot think of any instance when so much space in a newspaper has ever been given over to a group of academics. This, again, marks out this book as being highly unusual; indeed in many ways it represents a first in world terms, and I think that Wales can be proud of this collaborative achievement between academia and the press.

Initial discussions between the *Western Mail* and HRW focused on the possibility of writing a general, beginning-to-end, history of Wales. But this idea was soon abandoned. Outstanding books offering an overview of Welsh history have already been published by distinguished scholars such as John Davies, Geraint H. Jenkins, and others listed in the 'Suggestions for Further Reading' to be found at the end of the volume. For us to have attempted something similar would have been a somewhat futile exercise, almost doomed to failure because of the excellence of the works already published.

Instead, we decided to ask our historians to focus on a myth or misunderstanding in Welsh history, and then explore it in an attempt to create a 'new history of Wales'; that is, a history that challenges popular perceptions of our collective past. We were not seeking to provoke controversy for controversy's sake, but rather attempting to get beyond the one-dimensional views of the past that are so often to be found in popular histories and on television. The past is a complex place and part of the task of the historian is to interpret and explain that complexity for the benefit of public audiences. Thus, readers expecting to find a complete history of Wales in the pages that follow are going to be disappointed.

What they will find is 24 essays, some of which explore well-known issues or themes. Other essays find their way down the less familiar avenues and by-ways of Welsh history. Of course, some subjects and topics are conspicuous by their absence from the volume, but there was only so much ground that could be covered (and this leaves plenty of scope for a future series or two). We very much hope that readers will find this approach fresh, interesting, and above all thought-provoking, as we reflect upon our individual and collective identities, and the meaning of modern Wales.

To a lesser or greater extent, the past always informs the direction of travel of any nation, and as Wales tries to makes its way in a fast-changing and often dangerous world it is important that we all have a firm understanding of how we have arrived at the point where we are today. Our individual journeys have brought us all together in the present day from often very different starting points, but we are bound up together in a shared, collective past that is the history of Wales. We certainly need to celebrate that past but we also need to be critical of it; and the best way to be critical is by asking intelligent questions.

Such questions have been asked in this volume, and they have been answered (if only in part) by those best placed to do so: the leading experts in their fields.

The essays that follow are substantially as they appeared in the *Western Mail* in September and October 2010, and they are arranged in the order in which they were published. Some minor errors have been corrected by the authors, and the text has been re-formatted, but, apart from that, very few interventions have been made by the Editor.

Huw Bowen, Swansea, St David's Day 2011

1

HOW CELTIC ARE THE WELSH?

Raimund Karl

THE MYTH OF THE EUROPEAN CELTIC ORIGIN AND MIGRATION INTO BRITAIN

In the early 18th century, the Welsh antiquarian Edward Lhuyd discovered that several of the languages spoken in western Britain were closely related to a language spoken in antiquity. This language had been spoken in ancient Britain and Gaul. According to Caesar, those who spoke this language in Gaul called themselves, in their own tongue, *Celtae*. Thus, the idea of the Celtic origin of the Welsh was born.

In the late 19th and early 20th century, archaeological discoveries seemed to indicate that these ancient Celts did not just share a language, but also a material culture: similar types of finds were made across wide areas of Europe. Archaeologists classified these finds into two groups (see quote V.G. Childe 1929), named after two prominent find-spots in central Europe: the earlier Hallstatt culture (after a site in Austria), and the later La Tène culture (after a site in Switzerland). The latter, distributed across much of later prehistoric Europe, was seen as the direct descendant of the less widely distributed former. Also, the distribution of the latter seemed to coincide quite closely with the distribution of Celtic languages in antiquity.

EDWARD
LHUYD
1660-1709
IEITHYDD
HYNAFIAETHYDD
NATURIAETHWR

THE ANCIENT AND MODERN CELTIC LANGUAGES

Ancient Continent: Gaulish (France), Celtiberian (Spain), East Celtic (Central Europe), Lepontic (Northern Italy), Galatian (Turkey)

Ancient Britain: Ancient British/Brythonic (England/Wales/Southern Scotland), Ancient Gaelic/Goidelic (Ireland, Man, Western Scotland), Pictish ? (North-Eastern Scotland)

Modern Celtic languages: Welsh, Breton, Cornish (from Brythonic), Irish Gaelic, Scots Gaelic, Manx (from Goidelic)

'We find certain types of remains – pots, implements, ornaments, burial rites and house forms – constantly recurring together. Such a complex of associated traits we shall term a "cultural group" or just a "culture". We assume that such a complex is the material expression of what today would be called a "people".'

Vere Gordon Childe: definition of an archaeological culture (1929)

In the (nationalistic) spirit of that time, a simple explanation for these facts presented itself: a people (or even race) called 'Celts' originated in the Hallstatt culture of Central Europe, c1000BC. At c600BC, 'Hallstatt finds' start to appear in Britain, indicating an expansion of these continental Celts into Britain, presumably by means of military conquest. This seemed to be supported by the emergence of hill forts in the British archaeological record at roughly that time – Celtic warriors from the continent arrive, building 'castles' to control the conquered lands.

Somewhat later, at c450BC, the European Celts develop a new type of material expression, the La Tène culture. They become even more expansive during that phase: La Tène finds, it was believed, appear in Britain from c300BC onwards, indicating a second wave of a 'Celtic conquest' of Britain. A third, 'Belgian' conquest of south-eastern England seemed to follow at c150–100BC, seemingly even historically attested by Caesar in his 'Gaulish War'.

At roughly the same times, historical sources from the Mediterranean indicate Celtic conquests in the south, too: according to Livy, Celts from across the Alps were conquering Northern Italy c600BC and later, c390BC, even sacked Rome. And they were also expanding towards the south-east: they attacked Greece in c280BC, with part of their army crossing the Dardanelles and later establishing the Galatian kingdom in central Anatolia (modern Turkey).

All the evidence seemed to fit together nicely: Celtic warriors from Central Europe seemed to have conquered large parts of Europe between the sixth and first century BC. Those who made it to Wales, so the theory goes, became the ancestors of the Welsh, who stubbornly refused to be subjected to foreign rule even long after their continental cousins had succumbed to either the Romans or various Germanic invaders.

NOT SO SIMILAR AFTER ALL: NO CELTS IN BRITAIN?

Yet, in the last few decades, archaeologists have increasingly rejected this model: only if looked at very superficially, the evidence seems to support this model. If examined in greater detail, little remains of the 'Celtic invasion model'.

British 'La Tène', for instance, while showing some continental influences, clearly is very different from Continental La Tène: there are some similarities in the decoration of items and the motives used. But the items which are decorated are very much in a local tradition. Also, there are vast differences in

14

other aspects of material culture: while there are many La Tène cemeteries known from Continental Europe, there are hardly any in Britain (and those which do exist are restricted to very limited areas like east Yorkshire, and even there, rites differ distinctively from those observed on the continent). And while pretty much all Iron Age houses and many settlements on the Continent are more or less rectangular, most houses and settlements in Britain are more or less round. In fact, wherever one looks, difference to the Continent seems to be the rule, while similarity is the (rare) exception.

Thus, modern archaeology has moved away from the idea of the 'Celtic invaders' conquering Britain, and also from the idea that 'the Celts' were the ancestors of the Welsh. There is no evidence for a late prehistoric invasion from the Continent (let alone for three). Rather, all evidence seems to point at a local, thoroughly British origin of the people who were to become the Welsh.

'When considering the various sorts of society which have been termed 'Celtic', it is clear from the archaeology that there is an enormous range, from the urbanised societies of Gaul in the first century BC to the decentralised societies of the English Pennines; from the highly stratified societies represented in the burials from Vix and Hochdorf, to societies where it is difficult to pick out any prestige material goods.'

John R. Collis: different 'Celtic' societies (1994)

THE LATE BRONZE AGE – RELATIVES AND HOUSEHOLDS

While the actual 'origins' of the Welsh go much further back in time, the late Bronze Age (c1200–600BC) seems to have been a particularly important period: while before, much labour seems to have been invested into communal activities (like the construction of communal burial mounds and ritual monuments), individual settlements and the enclosure of land now seem to become the focus of labour investment. Settlements, including small farms, at first are enclosed by palisades and later with banks and even quite substantial ramparts. Ownership and control of land seems to become increasingly important during this period.

The Welsh language may give us some hints at what was happening during this period: kinship, i.e. (biological) descent from a common ancestor seems to have been a significant factor in social relations: *cenedl*, today meaning 'nation', originally probably referred to such a common-descent group, with different ranks within such a kin probably being mainly age-related. However, the increasing importance of the settlement community, the 'household' has also left its mark: the modern Welsh term for family, *teulu*, originally must have referred to the (male) members of a household (Celtic *teges-slougos* literally translates as 'house-troop').

Wider kin-groups, consisting of several different households, probably

Castell Henllys, a reconstructed Iron Age settlement

controlled only very small territories: perhaps a couple of square kilometres, perhaps as much as a valley or other naturally defined pocket of arable land. And while they probably intermarried and had other relations with each other (e.g. exchanging raw materials like metal), each such kin-group will have largely been independent of others: in a way, each of them probably was a mini-nation, responsible for its own affairs and subject to no one else.

IRON AGE TRANSFORMATIONS – FROM KIN TO COUNTRY

The changes which began in the late Bronze Age seem to have continued and resulted in further changes during the Iron Age (c800BC–AD100). Particularly in the latter half of this period, more and more labour seems to be invested into settlement monumentality: while late Bronze and early Iron Age settlements were mostly enclosed with a single palisade, bank or rampart, later Iron Age settlements frequently are surrounded by two, three or even more banks or ramparts. Frequently, these are quite substantial constructions, requiring considerable amounts of labour to build. This indicates that some households were gaining control over more land and also over more human resources. It seems as if society was changing, even if perhaps only slowly.

The reasons for this change are anything but clear: suspicions range widely. It may have been that a climate crisis in the latest Bronze and early Iron Age caused increased competition between households for land to support themselves. It may be that changes in technology – from Bronze to Iron – made

MENTRAU ADCC
NMGW ENTERPRISES LTD
Croeso/Welcome

Sales Receipt

Date : 05 May 2012		14:28
Receipt: 00266675		
POS NMG ART		

1 x A New History of Wales	B	14.99

To Pay:	14.99
Tendered:	15.00
Change:	0.01

Payment Method(s)

Cash:	15.00

Rate Code	Excl	VAT	Inc
20.00 A	0.00	0.00	0.00
0.00 B	14.99	0.00	14.99

VAT registration: GB 783 4541 10

Diolch/Thank you

You can also shop online – go to:

www.museumwales.ac.uk/shop

old metal exchange networks obsolete and thus resulted in social change. It may even be that it was just the passing of time which created increasingly larger communities by intermarriage and other means of kin-group interaction. It may have been a combination of all these and other factors.

But whatever the reasons, some households seem to have gained increased control over land and labour. Again, the Welsh language may give us some hints at the results of these changes: some members of the community seem to have gained more and more influence and become heads not just of their kin-group, but of a community inhabiting a certain area of land. This can for instance be seen in the medieval Welsh term *brëyr*, 'lord, noble', which is derived from an earlier (Celtic) word *mrogi-rīx*, which can literally be translated as 'land-ruler, king of a country'.

During the later Iron Age, such small 'countries' – probably each no larger than a commote or at the most a *cantref* – may have slowly converged into larger units. Again, this may be hinted at by a Welsh term: *brenin*, 'king' is derived from Celtic *brigantinos*, 'one who is pre-eminent in his class' (presumably of *mrogi-rīges*, 'land-rulers'). These larger communities are the 'tribes' that the Romans encounter in the early first millennium AD when they conquer Wales.

THE ROMANO-BRITISH PERIOD – NATIVES AND FOREIGNERS

In many ways, the Romano-British period (c AD70–400) seems to have brought little change. Of course, Roman military installations were being built across the country, roads constructed, mines exploited and so on, and this certainly must have had an influence on society. But by and large, Rome seems to have cared little about how some provincials near the end of the world organised their own communities, as long as the expected tax revenue was coming in and no major rebellions took place. And in fact, Roman social organisation may not have been all that different from what the natives were doing anyway: large landed estates owned by a wealthy noble (who, if ambitious, got involved in politics) and tilled by semi-dependant tenants or even slaves is pretty much how 'classical' Roman society was structured; and late Iron Age societies in Wales may well have functioned very similar to that. Thus, neither natives nor foreigners may have had to change much, even if the odd foreigner came in to take over an estate somewhere in Wales.

Roman influence thus seemingly mainly affected what Rome was interested in: the upper echelons of local administration. The formerly quasi-independent land rulers of the Iron Age were downgraded to mere nobles, subjects to the local ruler rather than his somewhat less eminent equivalents.

17

The formerly constantly shifting tribes of the Iron Age were consolidated into stable communities, the administrative districts (*civitates*) of Roman Wales, thus giving these territorial units a fixed historical pedigree of some 400 years – and thus long term stability even after the end of the Roman occupation of Britain. And the administration of these units became more or less formalised, again hinted at by the fact that the term for the court office in medieval Wales, *swydd*, is derived from a Latin rather than a 'native Celtic' word (see box Welsh terms).

The *cromlech* at Pentre Ifan, a Bronze Age burial chamber

BECOMING WELSH

Even after the end of the Roman occupation, Wales was not Wales yet. Rather, it consisted of several competing kingdoms, at first (and partially more or less consistently) closely following the territorial divisions established by the Roman administrative districts. Partially, Iron Age hill forts were reoccupied and remodelled into new 'royal seats', perhaps in a conscious attempt to connect to distant 'royal' ancestors before Rome had arrived. Due to conquest, intermarriage and other political means, territories started to shift more than during the Romano-British period again. Yet, if anything, the Welsh were not yet considering themselves to be Welsh, but rather British, and were anything but united or a nation.

In a sense, it was the English (or perhaps more precisely, the Mercians) who created Wales: in the eighth century, advances by (mainly) Mercia cut off the connection (at least by land) with other communities who considered themselves, and were considered by the inhabitants of what was to become Wales, as British. Only now, the Welsh shared one country with only the Welsh, thus becoming the *Cymry*. Similarly, only now those speaking English increasingly started to restrict the use of their generic term for 'foreigners', *wealhas*, to those who were, slowly but surely, becoming the Welsh.

Thus, today, it is no longer possible to maintain the myth that the Welsh are the descendants of some invading 'Celtic warriors' who for a while dominated much of Europe. Rather, the Welsh emerged from thoroughly local roots, by coming together to form a community, rather than by splitting from a common Celtic people.

WELSH TERMS

brenin: today meaning 'king', this is derived from Celtic *brigantinos*, 'pre-eminent in his class'

brëyr: medieval term for 'lord, noble', this is derived from Celtic *mrogi-rīx*, 'land-ruler, king of a country'

bro: today meaning 'area, district', this is derived from Celtic *mrogi-*, 'territory, country'

cenedl: today meaning 'nation', this is derived from Celtic *kenetlom*, 'kin-group, descendants of a common ancestor', compare Old Irish *cenél*, 'lineage, descent group, descendants of'

Cymru: Wales, derived from Brythonic *com-brogi*, 'sharing a land, countrymen'

swydd: today meaning 'job, post', this term referred to an office in the royal household in medieval Wales and derives from Latin *sēdes*, 'seat' (presumably in the *curia*, the council of a Roman district)

taeog: today meaning 'churl', this term referred to the 'tenant' in the Middle Ages and is derived from Celtic *teges-ākos*, 'dependant member of the house'

teulu: today meaning 'family', this is derived from Celtic *teges-slougos*, 'house-troop'

Inside an Iron Age roundhouse at Castell Henllys

2

WE WERE THE CELTS WHO FOUGHT THE ROMANS, WEREN'T WE?

Ray Howell

When my book *Searching for the Silures, an Iron Age tribe in south-east Wales* was first published, it led to a feature on the theme of Celts and Romans in the *Western Mail*.

The piece, by Sam Burson, picked up on the dominance of the colour red in the various bits of Iron Age metal work, particularly horse trappings, found in South Wales. The peg was an impending Wales-Italy international with Celts vs Romans providing an inviting comparison for Wales vs Italy and red harness-fittings going well with red rugby jerseys. Both Sam and I knew full well that you can't present today's red jerseys as an example of cultural continuity drawn from the red adorning Silurian chariots! Nevertheless, it was a nice link to the game and has, no doubt, boosted sales of the book.

However, the theme highlights some interesting issues. How much cultural continuity can we actually demonstrate in Wales? Is it appropriate to use the Celts vs Romans analogy? There is no question about the ferocity of Silurian resistance to the Roman invasion. The Roman historian Tacitus gives us graphic accounts of the Silurian War, a quarter of a century-long guerrilla conflict. But were these people Celts? Is it right to describe the Iron Age tribes of Wales as Celtic at all? Many argue that it isn't.

In the vanguard of the 'anti-Celts' is John Collis, professor of archaeology at Sheffield, who once wrote that there were no Celts in Britain. His argument was largely based on Caesar's description of his campaigns in Gaul, modern France, where he described three native groups, the Belgae, Aquitani and Celtoi. Collis thought that the description Celt should apply only very specifically to these particular Gaulish people.

Not everyone agreed. Many pointed to common cultural markers like La Tène design which permeated Europe during the later Iron Age. Patterns which were fashionable in Wales were also favoured in France, Austria and beyond. If we accept this as evidence of common culture, we need a word to describe it and Celtic is widely used to do just that.

The Celt sceptics responded by pointing to ways that material culture, the bits people leave behind and the basis of archaeology, can and can't be used. A popular analogy refers to the fact that wearing a baseball hat and drinking Coca Cola does not make someone an American. Similarly, decorating objects with La Tène patterns does not necessarily make someone a Celt.

Nevertheless, not using the term causes difficulties. One problem is that we have been using it for a long time. Antiquarians like William Stukeley were instrumental in imbedding the Celts in the popular imagination. In 1723, he described 'the Manner of Celtic Temples', believing that sites like Avebury and Stonehenge were built by 'the Celts'.

Even more to the point, is the fact that we need a term to describe the relationship between languages which developed in the European Iron Age. There are obvious links between languages like Gaulish and Old British and for many years those linkages have been described as Celtic. If we choose not to use that term, we will need to think of another.

Current thinking has recently been summed up nicely by John Koch of the University of Wales Centre for Advanced Welsh and Celtic Studies. In the 2009 edition of *Studia Celtica*, he wrote about 'Celts calling themselves Celts'. Referring to a recent lecture by Gaelic expert Kim McCone titled 'The Celtic Question', he addressed that very issue. It turns out that, linguistically, a range of people all across Gaul and others like the Celtiberians of Spain used the description Celt. Most importantly, there is also good evidence that the 'pre-Roman linguistic ancestors of the Britons and the Gaels (Irish) had once called themselves Celtoi'.

The consequence of this is that, as a language descriptor, it is fine for us to talk about British Celts. What's more, in Wales, probably more than in any other part of the British Isles, language is an obvious link to these early people. When we speak Welsh, we are not speaking the language of the Silures. But we are speaking a language which, despite strong influences of Latin and other languages, derives from theirs. We are speaking a 'Celtic language'.

Language is a part of Welsh cultural inheritance. Inevitably that encourages us to ask whether there are other aspects of continuity which can be found? When we look closely, it appears that there may be many.

The remains of Carn Ffoi, an Iron Age hill fort, on the slopes of Carn Ingli

THE SILURIAN WAR

My study of the Silures offers several cases in point. The Silures were the Iron Age people of south-east Wales, basically today's Glamorgan and Gwent. They, like other tribal groups including the Ordovices in North Wales and the Demetae in the west, made up the population of Wales on the eve of the Roman invasion.

Almost certainly a clan-based tribal confederation, the Silures put up fierce resistance to the Roman assault. They were initially led by Caratacus (Caradog), a prince of the Catuvellauni, the most powerful tribe in what is today south-east England. After a pitched battle, probably fought somewhere in Powys, Caratacus was eventually captured and packed off as a prisoner to Rome. There he made his famous speech before the Emperor, saving his life in the process.

Remarkably for the Silures, the loss of their war leader had little effect. In fact, Tacitus tells us that, if anything, they became even more ferocious in the aftermath. 'Battle followed battle,' the Roman historian wrote. These were often 'lightning strikes' in the woods as the Silures picked off small bands of Roman soldiers.

The Governor, Ostorius Scapula, died and Tacitus was sure that it was down to the strain of the protracted guerrilla war with the Silures. When the general Manlius Valens tried to defeat the tribe himself before the arrival of the new governor, the Silures massed and defeated the legion!

The people who mounted this remarkable quarter-century long resistance have, surprisingly, attracted less interest from archaeologists and historians than might be expected. Now, however, we are slowly gaining a better understanding of their society.

HORSES, WHEELS AND THE COLOUR RED

Much valuable work has been undertaken in the National Museum of Wales with Adam Gwilt and Mark Lodwick in particular providing insights from finds, many coming into the museum as a result of the Portable Antiquities Scheme. This is why we are seeing an increasing amount of metal work from the region including the red-enamelled horse-trappings which inspired the story in the *Western Mail.*

These objects are beginning to tell us a great deal about the Silures. For a start, horses were important in their society. There is more. Among the objects are terrets, metal rings which had only one use. Terrets were to feed through reins. That means that they were using wheeled vehicles. In the terrain of South Wales, that means something else. They would have needed to make roads!

The sophistication which this suggests fits in well with current research which I am undertaking with Giles Oatley of UWIC. Using computer-based mapping systems to look at the Iron Age hill forts of the area, we are examining things like viewsheds, what you could have seen when you looked from the ramparts of the hill forts, and line of sight, addressing issues like which hill forts you can see from other hill forts.

It is early days but it is already obvious that you won't find a hill fort from which you can't see at least one other. It is also clear that hill forts in the region are located in clusters. It all suggests a complex and sophisticated society with skilled craftsmen and cultural cohesion, even if primarily within the clan groupings suggested by the clustering. Perhaps it is no surprise that they resisted the Romans so effectively for so long!

ROMAN OCCUPATION

Eventually, however, they were defeated. Tacitus wrote that the governor Julius Frontinus finally defeated the Silures, overcoming 'the valour of his enemy and the difficulty of the terrain', in about AD75. He ordered the building of the legionary fortress in Caerleon which became the military and administrative centre for the whole of South Wales and the West Country. Military occupation of the Silurian region had begun.

To search for evidence of continuity, we must ask what happened next. What sort of relationship developed between the Romans and the Silures? To answer that question, it is important to think about Caerwent.

The Roman remains in Caerleon and Caerwent are among the most impressive history/heritage sites in Wales. They are also hugely important in helping us to understand Romano-British society in Wales. This is particularly true of Caerwent, the civitas capital of the Silures.

Civitas administration was basically a form of devolution. The system was employed throughout the Roman Empire with a range of government functions devolved to local authorities. That usually meant devolved to tribes. For the Romans this was not so much a question of improved government as of shifting burdens like tax collection onto local communities. Nevertheless, it became an important factor in tribal survival.

Caerwent, Venta Silurum or the Market of the Silures to the Romans, became the devolved capital of the tribe. A key question is when civitas administration began because that says a great deal about the relationship between natives and Romans. A civitas was governed by an *ordo*, a sort of tribal senate. Generally, an ordo would sit in a basilica, often built in the centre of the capital. There is just such a basilica in Caerwent. It follows that if we can date the construction of the basilica, we are well placed to say when the civitas was created.

Our understanding of Roman Caerwent has improved dramatically as a result of research excavations directed by Richard Brewer, Keeper of Archaeology in the National Museum. Amongst other sites, Richard and his team have excavated the basilica and a portion of the forum in Caerwent. They were able to date the construction of the building which was Hadrianic, in other words, built in the 120s.

The Roman amphitheatre at Caerleon

The newly excavated bath complex at Caerleon in 1979

This makes a great deal of sense. Half a century is probably just about enough time for tensions generated in a protracted guerrilla war to subside. Besides, by then the Romans had other things on their mind. The fact that the basilica was Hadrianic reminds us that it was built at a time when the Emperor was defining borders. In Britain, it was the period when large numbers of troops, including members of the Second Augustan Legion normally billeted in Caerleon, were moved north to build Hadrian's Wall. For the Romans, that would have been a good time to shift some responsibilities onto local communities.

CULTURAL CONFLATION

It seems that at least elements of the Silurian aristocracy accepted the new Roman order. A telling piece of evidence is the 'Paulinus stone' now in the church porch in Caerwent. Dedicated to a Legate of the Second Augustan legion, its inscription proclaims in good Latin that it was erected on the authority of the ordo of the Silures. Many people point to the inscription as clear evidence that the Silures had embraced Roman practices. However, I always counsel caution to my students. It also confirms that they were still identifying themselves as Silures in the early third century.

Also in the porch of the church is a small altar. Its inscription tells us something else. It is a dedication to the god Mars-Ocelus. Mars was the Roman god of war. Ocelus was a native deity with similar attributes. Here we have a wonderful example of cultural conflation. Native and Classical, Celt and Roman – the two deities have been fused into one entity.

There are other sculptures from Caerwent which remind us of something else. A seated mother-goddess must have been revered in the Roman town, but she has few Roman qualities. A stone head excavated from a fourth century level has no Roman qualities at all. Nevertheless, it had been placed at one end of a narrow corridor on a raised platform which must have been an altar. As Roman Britain was drawing to an end, this purely native object was being venerated in the civitas capital!

The picture which emerges is one of a mixed and no doubt vibrant culture with native tradition playing an important part in a multi-cultural society. If native Silurian culture was strong in the civitas capital, every indication is that it was even stronger in the countryside. Sites like Thornwell Farm near Chepstow are a case in point. Excavations there by Gwilym Hughes, now Cadw's chief inspector of ancient monuments, showed that people were living in roundhouses right through the Roman era. The roundhouses of the Iron Age are frequently seen as indicators of native tradition. Their continued use throughout the fourth century seems to confirm the resilience of that tradition.

A model which we have is one of survival of the traditional cultures of tribal groupings like the Silures to the end of the Romano-British period and beyond. With the end of Roman Britain, small kingdoms emerged. These kingdoms were born at a time that we can accurately describe as the emergence of Wales.

In south-east Wales, the early kingdom was called Gwent. We have documentary evidence which names some of the early kings of the region. It is fascinating that the earliest of the named kings of Gwent was Caradog Freichfas. Caradog is the Welsh form of Caratacus. The name of the great resistance leader at the beginning of the Silurian War was not only remembered in the fifth century. It was clearly thought a name worthy of a king!

Even more important is the name of his kingdom. Roman Venta Silurum was being described in the vernacular language as the fortress of Venta, Caerwent. That in turn gave its name to the new kingdom – Gwent! The people of the region were speaking a Latinized language, but at its heart was the earlier linguistic tradition of the Iron Age. They were speaking a very early form of Welsh.

They, like many of us today, were speaking what we can confidently describe as a Celtic language – and language may be the most important cultural indicator of all.

3

LLYWELYN THE GREAT AND LLYWELYN THE LAST – FOR THEMSELVES OR FOR WALES?

Huw Pryce

In the 13th century the princes of Gwynedd achieved extensive domination over Wales. One of them, Llywelyn ap Gruffudd, even succeeded in getting the king of England to recognize him as Prince of Wales, ruling the other Welsh lords in a principality of Wales. But were the princes aiming at all-out independence, or rather a medieval equivalent of devolution?

On the landing of Cardiff City Hall is a series of marble statues commemorating Welsh heroes unveiled by David Lloyd George in 1916. One of these strikes a defiant pose, with his right arm raised and his head held high: Llywelyn ap Gruffudd or Llywelyn the Last, the prince of Wales killed on December 11, 1282. Llywelyn's

Statue of Llywelyn ap Gruffudd

death has often been seen as ending all hopes for Welsh independence. To quote the on-line encyclopedia 'Wikipedia', Llywelyn was 'the last prince of an independent Wales before its conquest by Edward I of England'. There's certainly an important grain of truth in this view. The prince's death in 1282 did, after all, effectively mark the end of a Welsh tradition of political rule that originated in the vacuum created by the withdrawal of Roman forces from Britain almost 900 years earlier. (Owain Glyndŵr's attempt to renew that tradition in the early 1400s, though remarkably successful to begin with, ended in failure.)

On the other hand, it's an oversimplification to think that Llywelyn ruled, or even wanted to establish, an independent Wales. The same is largely true of earlier 13th-century princes of Gwynedd, notably his grandfather Llywelyn ap Iorwerth or Llywelyn the Great (d.1240). As recent scholarship has shown, notably Professor J. Beverley Smith's magisterial biography of Llywelyn ap Gruffudd, such an assessment claims both too much and too little for what these rulers were trying to do.

Too much, because there was no prospect of any 13th-century Welsh ruler being fully independent of the king of England. But also too little, because an emphasis on the single issue of independence can lead us to lose sight of the bigger – and more complex – picture of the princes' aims and achievements.

LLYWELYN THE GREAT AND THE KING OF ENGLAND

Since the Anglo-Saxon period, English kings had claimed overlordship over Welsh rulers. Moreover, those claims had been accepted by some Welsh kings: for example, Hywel Dda (Hywel the Good; d.950) submitted to Athelstan (d.939), the first king of England, and attended his court. After 1066 the Norman and Plantagenet kings of England inherited this tradition of overlordship and defined it more sharply than before. Submission now took the form of a special oath of allegiance (fealty), often reinforced by a ceremony of homage in which the Welsh ruler acknowledged that he held his lands from the king and thus became his vassal. In addition, down to 1267 kings of England insisted that all Welsh rulers owed fealty and homage individually. Accordingly they strongly resisted the ambitions of the princes of Gwynedd to offer submission on behalf of all the other Welsh princes and lords – something which would have amounted to recognizing the authority of the princes of Gwynedd over a wider Welsh polity: a principality of Wales.

Llywelyn the Great never claimed to be 'Prince of Wales' and was never recognized as such by the English crown. (Interestingly, though, at the end of her life his foreign wife Joan (d.1237), the illegitimate daughter of King John, implicitly articulated her husband's wider ambitions by using the title 'Lady of Wales'.) In his early years a formal relationship with the crown was a way of cementing Llywelyn's position against dynastic rivals. In an agreement with the representatives of King John in July 1201, Llywelyn swore to observe fealty to the king, received all his lands from the king's justiciar (deputy) and promised to do homage to John when he returned from the Continent. These terms might seem demeaning. But they gave the prince vital recognition from a power that could otherwise have stopped him from securing his hold on Gwynedd – either by backing rival claimants or, at worst, by sending royal forces against him. The dangers of the latter scenario became all too clear ten years later, when John led a devastatingly effective campaign against Gwynedd that ended in Llywelyn's unconditional surrender.

It's true that the prince bounced back remarkably quickly, and went on to expand his authority as the head of a military coalition that inflicted major reverses on the Crown and the Marcher lords across much of Wales. Yet this didn't lead to a bid for outright independence. What Llywelyn probably hoped for was to be recognized as the dominant Welsh ruler who alone would give homage to the Crown on behalf of his coalition allies. However, in peace talks at Worcester in March 1218 the regents governing on behalf of King John's ten-year-old son and successor, Henry III (1216–72), stuck hard to the principle that

Strata Florida, site of the Council of Welsh Princes in 1238.

all Welsh rulers owed homage to the king. What's more, while obtaining some important concessions, Llywelyn ended up promising to try to get those rulers to do precisely that.

DAFYDD AP LLYWELYN AND THE POPE

Llywelyn maintained his position of supremacy for the rest of his life. However, he was unable to ensure that his supremacy continued after his death in April 1240. What happened next is a good example of how kings of England took advantage of disputed successions in order to assert their rights of overlordship.

Llywelyn had gone to great lengths to establish his son Dafydd – born to his wife Joan – as his successor. Both the marriage and the plans for succession were examples of broader attempts by the 13th-century rulers of Gwynedd to modernize by forging closer ties with, and imitating, their neighbours, especially in England. One aim here was to enhance the prince's status and strengthen him vis-à-vis other Welsh lords. Thus by marrying Joan, Llywelyn established a special relationship with the powerful Plantagenet dynasty. And, as in England at the time – but in contrast to previous Welsh custom – he made legitimate birth an essential qualification for succession: Llywelyn got the Pope to recognize Dafydd as his successor, rather than his elder son Gruffudd, on the grounds that Gruffudd had been born out of wedlock. Dafydd duly succeeded, but when a month later he gave homage to his uncle, Henry III, it was only for 'North Wales' or Gwynedd. The Crown denied the new prince the right to succeed to the wider authority in Wales his father Llywelyn had enjoyed. The reason for this was simple. Gruffudd enjoyed considerable support in Gwynedd: many felt that he had been unfairly passed over and had at least as much right as Dafydd to succeed Llywelyn. Dafydd had to make sure that the king confirmed him as successor rather than backing his brother.

Dynastic divisions thus gave the king the upper hand. Yet Dafydd clearly hoped to follow in his father's footsteps and extend his power far beyond Gwynedd. Indeed this half-Welsh prince arguably went further than either of the Llywelyns in trying to create a principality of Wales independent of the king of England. In the end, however, that attempt only served to underline the domination of the English Crown.

Dafydd was freed to make his bid for independence by the removal of the dynastic threat. The prince had captured Gruffudd in the autumn of 1240, but had been forced to hand him over to the king after a royal campaign against Gwynedd the following summer. However, on St David's Day 1244, Gruffudd plunged to his death while trying to escape from the Tower of London. By the summer, Dafydd, in alliance with other Welsh princes, had launched widespread attacks across Wales.

Most dramatic of all, the prince tried to by-pass the king of England by becoming a vassal of the Pope. According to Matthew Paris, the well-informed English historian writing at this time, 'Dafydd, intending to free his neck from the yoke of fealty to the lord king, took flight to the wings of papal protection, pretending that he held a part of Wales from the Pope directly. The Pope was favourable to him.' Paris also reports that Dafydd agreed to pay the Pope a tribute of 500 marks (about £330) a year. It wasn't unusual for secular rulers to seek papal protection in this way. The kings of Bohemia, Croatia and Portugal as well as the ruler of the Isle of Man had already done so. But Dafydd's success was short-lived. In April 1245, after an inquiry, Pope Innocent IV reversed his decision to recognize the prince as his vassal. It was well known, he said, that Dafydd's ancestors had always been vassals of the king of England. As Michael Richter has argued, the Pope couldn't afford to antagonize Henry III, whose support he needed in his ongoing struggles with the Emperor Frederick II. Dafydd's bold bid for independence fell victim to higher priorities in papal diplomacy.

THE TREATY OF MONTGOMERY 1267

Despite this setback Dafydd continued to wage war in defiance of Henry III, but died, still a young man, in February 1246. Some two decades later, in September 1267, the papacy found itself once again involved in Welsh affairs. However, this was no repeat of the attempt to leapfrog, as it were, over the king of England and submit instead to Rome. Rather, the Pope's representative in England, Cardinal Ottobuono, acted as a mediator in negotiations between Henry III and Dafydd's nephew and eventual successor, Llywelyn ap Gruffudd.

The result of those negotiations was the Treaty of Montgomery. This treaty marked an important milestone in the history of medieval Wales. For the first time, the king of England recognized a Welsh ruler as Prince of Wales, ruling a principality of Wales and having the right to receive homage from the other Welsh princes and lords. At the same time, the clerks who drafted the treaty were very careful to stress that the prince and his principality were created by the Crown and remained subject to it. Though Llywelyn had been described as 'Prince of Wales' in one document as early as 1258, and had regularly used this title since 1262, the Treaty of Montgomery gives him no title in the opening clauses that deal with territorial disputes. Then we read: 'The Lord King of England, wishing to magnify the person of Llywelyn and in him honour the others who lawfully succeed him, by his pure liberality and grace, and with the assent and will of his eldest born son the Lord Edward, gives and concedes to the aforesaid Llywelyn and his heirs the Principality of Wales, so that the same Llywelyn and his heirs may be called and are Princes of Wales.' Moreover, this act of liberality came with strict conditions and at a heavy cost, as Llywelyn agreed to give homage and fealty to the king and also pay him 25,000 marks (over £16,600) in instalments. The first payment of 5,000 marks (over £3,000) may have been almost as much as the prince's entire annual income, and the financial burdens created by the agreement contributed to major political difficulties in the following years.

MILITARY EXPANSION AND POLITICAL SPIN

Why was Llywelyn willing to spend so much on a title? After all, his grandfather, Llywelyn the Great, had enjoyed extensive power in Wales without ever being called Prince of Wales. The answer of course is that much more was at stake than simply a title. What Llywelyn ap Gruffudd wanted was a peace agreement that would give legitimacy to a new political structure that would last and be passed on to his successors: the principality of Wales. And he recognized that the king of England offered the best hope of providing this legitimacy and guaranteeing the principality's long-term future. For Llywelyn, then, the Treaty of Montgomery was a means of cementing the widespread authority he had established over the other Welsh princes and lords through military might. Rather than seeing it mainly in the context of relations between Wales and England, it is perhaps more helpful to view it from the perspective of Llywelyn's ambition to expand his power in Wales.

Whether the prince made the most of the treaty in order to fulfil his ambition is, admittedly, seriously open to question. In particular, despite the justifications he gave, Llywelyn clearly antagonized Henry III's successor Edward I by refusing to give him homage and by stopping the payments due under the treaty. This in turn helped to give the king a justification for launching a war in 1277 that resulted in the effective dismantling of the principality established only ten years earlier, though Llywelyn kept his title Prince of Wales until he was killed in Edward I's second Welsh war of 1282–83 which completed the English conquest of Wales.

What is clear is that Llywelyn was ready to talk up his status in ways that emphasized his authority rather than his obligations to the English Crown. A striking example appears in a letter addressed to Edward I in July 1273, following complaints that he had begun to build a castle at Dolforwyn near Montgomery.

The king knows well, Llywelyn wrote, 'that the rights of our principality are entirely separate from the rights of your kingdom although we may hold our principality under your royal power'. And, as Edward's forces closed in on Gwynedd a month before the prince's death, Llywelyn's council, in a rejection of peace proposals made by Archbishop Peckham of Canterbury, stressed that the principality was an ancient inheritance, implying that it owed nothing to the king of England. Evoking the legendary accounts of the Trojan descent of the Welsh, the council declared that the land of Snowdonia belonged to 'the appurtenances of the principality of Wales, which he [Llywelyn] and his predecessors held since time of Brutus, so it is said'.

However, this appeal to Brutus was a unique cry of defiance uttered in desperate times. In reality, the wider authority which the princes of Gwynedd achieved at various points in the 13th century was the result of their own military and diplomatic efforts. At the same time, though, both Llywelyn the Great and Llywelyn the Last recognized the need for an agreement with their overlord, the king of England, if a principality of Wales was to survive on a secure footing. It is, perhaps, one of the ironies of Welsh history that the principality granted by the Crown in 1267 to confirm the dominance achieved by Llywelyn ap Gruffudd did, indeed, survive Edward I's conquest – as a possession of the crown of England, granted to the monarch's eldest son. Yet the basis for this survival was arguably in the terms of the Treaty of Montgomery itself, which had left no doubt that the principality of Wales was a royal creation. Thus what had originated as a recognition of Welsh state-building became a means of legitimizing English rule in Wales.

Dolwyddelan Castle, a stronghold of the Princes of Gwynedd, built by Llywelyn the Great

4

WERE WE WELSH
OR WERE WE BRITISH?

Huw Pryce

Devolution has the potential for creating a Welsh civic identity, regardless of ethnic background. But how was Welsh identity seen in the past? Can its origins be traced back to the Middle Ages? Was there even such a thing as national identity in medieval Wales? Throughout the Middle Ages Wales lacked the political unity we associate with a modern nation-state, and the mountains and forests that covered much of its landscape made travel difficult. How could its people have had a sense of nationhood?

Despite not being a single political or administrative unit, however, it's clear that the inhabitants of medieval Wales were capable of feeling they belonged together as a distinctive people with the hallmarks of what we would call a nation. Admittedly that sense of belonging could be expressed in ways that seem surprising today. For one thing, in its most popular form it focused not on Wales, but Britain. And, when they did focus on Wales, Welsh authors writing in Latin usually used terms for the country and people first devised by the English.

MEDIEVAL NATIONHOOD IN THE MODERN WORLD

Recent studies of national identity in medieval Wales are part of a much wider reassessment of the extent to which a sense of nationhood existed in medieval Europe. Indeed it was a Welsh historian, the late Rees Davies, who did much to promote this reassessment through his work on Wales as well as on Ireland, Scotland and England. In arguing that national identity was a medieval reality, Professor Davies and likeminded scholars responded to larger debates about the origins of modern nations and nationalism. In particular, they questioned the influential view that the nation is essentially a modern phenomenon. According

Statue of Owain Glyndŵr

to this view, modern ideas of nationhood might draw on elements like language, literature or even political structures that went back to the Middle Ages. Yet those elements were combined and given a new meaning in the very different world that emerged after the American and French revolutions of the late 18th century.

Of course, medieval historians accept that national identity was not the same in the Middle Ages as it was in the modern period. For instance, in the medieval world a sense of common nationhood couldn't be promoted through mass media or mobilized as a political movement – nationalism – within a broader process of democratization.

Nor do medieval historians necessarily assume that any medieval sense of nationhood survived unchanged to form the basis of national identity in the modern era. Indeed on the whole they don't simply assume national identity existed in medieval societies. Yet, they would argue, neither should we assume that it could not have existed in those societies. Accordingly, they are interested in finding out how far national identity may be detected and the contexts in which it was articulated.

Their approach is thus very different from that of Welsh historians a century or so ago such as O. M. Edwards and J. E. Lloyd, who took for granted that Wales became a nation in the Middle Ages. What's more, those earlier historians believed that the sense of nationhood created then had survived across the centuries and been reawakened in their own day – above all in the cultural and educational movements that led to the creation of national institutions like the University of Wales and the National Museum of Wales. One thing some medieval historians have tried to do is to debunk simplistic claims, often proclaimed loudest by nationalist politicians, that modern nations were created in the distant medieval past. Indeed the American medieval historian, Patrick Geary, has asserted that such thinking has created a 'toxic waste' whose poisonous effects have been all too evident in, for instance, the nationalism unleashed in the Balkan wars at the end of the twentieth century.

Historians, then, no longer see nationality as an almost timeless reality that originated in the Middle Ages and remained essentially the same until the present day. Yet medieval historians have also pointed out that people in the Middle Ages did have a sense of what looks very like national identity. This was based partly on a shared language and culture, often reinforced by a belief in common origins, and partly on a sense of belonging to a particular territory.

THE BRITISH PAST AND FUTURE

Both the ethnic and territorial aspects of identity are found in medieval Wales. But the situation is complicated because they were applied to two overlapping yet different arenas: Wales and Britain. How could the Welsh have felt they had a distinctively Welsh identity when their sense of belonging focused so strongly on the Britons and Britain? For most of the Middle Ages, sources written in or about Wales stress the notion that the Welsh were descended from the ancient Britons who had held sway over the island of Britain until the Anglo-Saxons displaced them. As the Anglo-Saxons established the kingdoms of what would become England, so the Britons were confined to the north and west of the island. (The English territorial term 'England' – or to use the form used then, 'Engla land' – became established in the early 11th century, possibly promoted deliberately by the Danish conqueror, King Cnut.) The most successful British kingdoms were those of Wales, and gradually the idea developed that their inhabitants represented the Britons who had once ruled over much of Britain. The Welsh were the true Brits.

What's more, this ancestry was made even more glorious by claiming that the Britons were in turn descended from the Trojans. These were one of the great peoples of classical antiquity, whose leader Aeneas was thought to have left Troy (in modern Turkey) for Italy and founded Rome. We first find this claim in a 'History of the Britons' written in Gwynedd about 830. This says that Britain was named after Brutus (or Britto), a descendant of Aeneas who had taken over the island and peopled it with his followers. Such origin legends were common in the Middle Ages – for instance, the Franks also claimed Trojan descent – and were designed to give prestige to the people concerned.

An important element in Welsh identity, then, was a sense of loss: the loss of Britain to the English. Linked to this, though, was the hope of recovering control of the island. It's true that Gildas, a sharp-tongued churchman writing around 540, thought the Britons had only got what they deserved. In his view, they had been justly punished by God for their sins. But for much of the medieval period a powerful tradition of prophecy, promoted by the poets, looked forward to the day when the Welsh would recover their British inheritance and drive out the English usurpers. In a sense, then, the Welsh were the first exponents of a British nationalism (just as, in Elizabeth I's reign, a man of Welsh origin, John Dee, was the first to use the term 'British Empire').

The passionately anti-English feeling underpinning such hopes of recovery are captured in the early Welsh poem '*Armes Prydein*' (The Prophecy of Britain), composed in the tenth century, probably in protest against the overlordship of the kings of England. This envisaged an alliance of the Welsh with the other Celtic-speaking peoples and the Vikings in Ireland which would drive the oppressive English out of Britain: 'When corpses stand up . . . / as far as the port of Sandwich – may it be blessed! / The foreigners (will be) starting for exile . . .'. It's likely that conflict with the English gave an extra edge to what today may sound like incitements to racial hatred: according to Gerald of Wales and others, they were widespread when the Welsh fought successfully against the Crown and the Marcher lords in the 12th century. In the end, though, the poets settled for a less cataclysmic fulfilment of these prophecies: the accession of the partly Welsh Henry Tudor to the throne of England in 1485.

WALES AND BRITAIN

The idea that Wales represented the remnant of the Britons' former sovereignty over Britain was expressed most strikingly by Welsh writers in Latin who called Wales 'Britain' ('Britannia'). Thus, after saying that 'all the districts of the southern region of "Britannia" belonged to King Alfred', Asser of St Davids, writing in the 890s, went on to list rulers in South Wales – not the south of England. In part, this usage, which lasted from Asser's time to the 1150s, gave territorial expression to the notion that the Welsh were still, essentially, Britons. But there may be a further implication, too: that Wales now *was* Britain as it was by far the largest remnant of the island that had once been held by the Britons.

There may also originally have been a British dimension to the Welsh word still used today for Wales and the Welsh: 'Cymry'. (The spelling 'Cymru' for the country is a later modification.) While the singular form 'Cymro' literally meant 'member of the same locality', in the period before the Norman conquest it was not applied exclusively to Wales. For instance, it was also used in the tenth century for the Britons of Strathclyde. It may even have been used in the same way as the Welsh term 'Brython' to mean the Britons in general, in the sense of speakers of a common British language known as 'Cymraeg'. But, as with the British terminology in Latin, the Welsh words came to be restricted to the people and territory of Wales.

We don't know when the idea of Wales as a distinct territory first emerged. If

Offa's Dyke

a poem praising Cadwallon, king of Gwynedd (d.634) was originally composed during the king's lifetime, 'Cymry' could already mean Wales at that time. As we've seen, the idea is certainly there in Asser in the 890s. His life of King Alfred of Wessex is the earliest source to mention Offa's Dyke, built on the orders of King Offa of Mercia (d.796). Later medieval Welsh sources present the dyke as marking the border between England and Wales, and it may have helped to define Wales as a territorial unit over and above the individual kingdoms into which it was divided.

WALES AND THE WELSH

The tiny minority of Welsh people able to write Latin started to call themselves 'Welsh' and their country 'Wales' in the 12th century. In doing this, they adapted Old English usage. (Like 'Cymry' in Welsh, Old English 'Wealas' – modern English 'Wales' – could mean both the country and the people.) The immediate stimulus probably came from the Normans, who, after their conquest of England, used forms of 'Wealas' and Latin derivatives like 'Wallia'. Quite possibly, unlike the Anglo-Saxons before them, the Normans found the older 'British' terminology too ambiguous, not least because it could apply to their neighbours in Brittany. The ambiguity was potentially all the greater as some Bretons took part in the conquest and settled in south-east Wales.

Old English 'Wealas' had originally signified a non-Germanic foreigner. Later, both Geoffrey of Monmouth and Gerald of Wales gave the term pejorative connotations: the Welsh were merely the bedraggled remnants of the once glorious Britons. Yet the Welsh clerics who adopted it in the 12th century clearly didn't think this. Quite the contrary: they gave the 'Welsh' terminology a new, sometimes defiant significance. After all, the Latinized term 'Wallia' came to express the Wales-wide ambitions of the most powerful princes. In their Latin documents, Owain Gwynedd (d.1170) and his descendant Llywelyn ap Gruffudd (d.1282) – and later Owain Glyndŵr (d.c.1415) – were given the title 'Prince of Wales'. What had once been a term of abuse became shorthand for political ambition.

Paradoxically, the idea of Wales as a distinctive territorial – and potential political – entity seems to have gained momentum precisely in the two centuries, from about 1093 to 1282, when sizeable parts of it were falling into the hands of Norman and English conquerors. Thus the compilers of the earliest surviving books of Welsh law, which date from this period, alleged that it was reformed by Hywel Dda (the Good), king or prince of 'all Wales', and stressed that it applied throughout Wales.

While court poets were stalwart upholders of the British inheritance of the Welsh, comparing the princes they praised with early British leaders fighting the Anglo-Saxons, they also asserted that some princes enjoyed authority over much or all of Wales. The network of Cistercian abbeys patronized by Welsh princes – extending from Whitland to Valle Crucis (Llangollen) and from Conwy to Caerleon – probably helped to reinforce a sense of belonging to a national community that transcended individual principalities. Monks at these abbeys wrote chronicles that projected a vision of a distinctive Welsh past. For instance, one wrote that in 1164 'all the Welsh of North Wales, South Wales and Powys unanimously threw off the yoke of the French'.

Such thinking made its way into political rhetoric. In 1282 Llewelyn ap Gruffudd, Prince of Wales, complained that 'we and all the Welsh' had been oppressed by English officials. Whether 'all the Welsh' would have agreed is beside the point. The prince's claim both reflected and reinforced the idea that the Welsh were a nation.

Valle Crucis

THE OLD MAN OF PENCADER – AMBIGUOUS VOICE OF A NATION?

'Whatever else may come to pass, I do not think that any people other than the Welsh, or any other language, will give answer on the Day of Direst Judgement to the Supreme Judge for this small corner of the earth.'

These were the words of an old man from Pencader (Carmarthenshire) according to Gerald of Wales at the end of his book *The Description of Wales* (1194). At first sight, this is a resounding vote of confidence in the future of the Welsh nation, one that assumes an inseparable link between people, language and territory. Yet read in the context of Gerald's book, the words take on a more ambivalent meaning. When Gerald was writing, the Lord Rhys and his sons were seizing castles and lands from the English Crown and marcher lords across a broad swathe of South Wales. Indeed some at court blamed Gerald, who was employed by the Crown, for failing to keep the peace and accused him of favouring Rhys, to whom he was related. It may be that Gerald hoped the book would prove his loyalty to the Crown by showing that the new-found confidence of the Welsh was built on sand.

To begin with, the old man of Pencader was a reminder of Welsh divisions, as we learn he had been a soldier in the army of King Henry II of England on a campaign in 1163 that ended with the Lord Rhys's capture. In addition, for all their apparent defiance, the old man's words fall far short of supporting the headiest hopes of the Welsh – namely that they would recover the sovereignty over Britain their British ancestors had lost to the English. Elsewhere in 'The Description' Gerald is emphatic that such hopes, though widely held by the Welsh, were completely unjustified. The reason was simple: they were far too sinful. Indeed, much of the second part of 'The Description' denounces their alleged failings. Therefore to say that the Welsh would survive in 'this small corner of the earth', meaning Wales, was to cut them down to size by implying they would never recover control over Britain. Even if the king couldn't conquer the Welsh completely, they were no great threat.

5

WHAT LAY BEHIND THOSE MONASTERY WALLS?

Janet Burton and Karen Stöber

If we ever think about medieval monasteries at all, we tend to conjure up images of seclusion, of monks or nuns in silence and prayer, cut off from the outside world and deeply immersed in their own spiritual lives. We tend to think of the religious houses of medieval Wales as peripheral, not just in the geographical sense, but also in the sense of their remoteness from the rest of medieval society. And we tend to think of ruins – picturesque ruins, that is.

Tintern Abbey

Turning off the A48 on our way to the Severn Bridge, for example, we pass the spectacular remains of the Cistercian abbey of Tintern. And normally, this is just what we do: we pass them, impressed, perhaps, by their grandeur, which is all the grander on account of their remoteness. But if we pause for a moment and think about what these places were like in their heyday, some 800 years ago, we will come to realise that far from remote and inward-looking, Tintern Abbey and the other 40-odd abbeys and priories of Wales during the Middle Ages were vibrant institutions that were really very much part of medieval society.

The histories of some of these abbeys can be reconstructed both from abundant documentary records such as charters, chronicles and formal correspondence. Others are better known for their architectural or archaeological remains. The ruins of Tintern Abbey, for instance, have attracted the attention – and admiration – of tourists since the 18th century. Moreover the unique poetry of the later medieval Welsh bards, especially men like Guto'r Glyn and Tudur Aled, allows us an insight into the perceptions of these important institutions, while a wide range of visual sources, including tombs, sculpture and heraldic tiles bear witness to the vibrant relationship between monastic houses and their patrons, those who offered them sustenance and protection.

AFTER THE NORMANS

When the Normans invaded and settled Wales from the late 11th century onwards, they transformed the native monasticism they found there, and began to introduce monastic houses of a type with which they were familiar on the continent and in England. According to the 12th-century monk William of Malmesbury, with the coming of the Normans to Britain you could see churches and monasteries rising up in every town and village, built in a 'style unknown before'. These new Benedictine priories were not just centres of prayer. As the newcomers pressed westwards they established monasteries as symbols of their power, often accompanied by another – the stone castle. Along the current A40 – at Monmouth, Abergavenny, Brecon, Llandovery and Carmarthen, for example – monasteries arose, their alien character made more obvious by the fact that they were dependent on, and enjoyed close links with, the monasteries in Normandy or England from which they had been founded. Over the course of the next hundred years or so the Benedictines were joined by houses of regular canons, of Cistercian monks, and of nuns, so that by the 13th century, medieval Wales had a lively monastic community in which all the major religious orders were represented.

POWERHOUSES OF PRAYER

So why did people found religious houses? The main purpose of the monastery was not just to provide its founder or patron with a glorified status symbol, but to furnish him or her, and others, with prayers. Medieval people believed firmly that their ultimate salvation would be aided by the intercessions of religious communities. Praised by the poets as 'God's temples', the monasteries and nunneries of medieval Wales were at the heart of the religious life of the country. In other words, they were in charge of the welfare of people's souls.

As members of international religious orders, they were also firmly integrated in a wide network of institutions dedicated to the praise of God and the spiritual welfare both of themselves and of society at large. A medieval man or woman who granted land to a monastery 'for the salvation of my soul' expected spiritual benefits in return for their generosity, and the prayers of monks, canons and nuns were therefore seen as central to the well ordering of the broader community.

But the role the religious communities of Wales played in their society extended far beyond the provision of spiritual services. These communities played an important and very involved part in the social, political and economic life of medieval Wales, as well as being centres of religion and learning.

SCHOLARSHIP AND LEARNING

There were no universities in medieval Wales. So where did people go to get an education?

Well, we know that for their contemporaries beyond the convent walls, the religious houses of the Principality were not only impressive edifices, 'mansions hemmed with lead and glass,' but they were also renowned for their education. Guto'r Glyn praised the 'good scholarship' and 'great learning' of the abbot of Strata Florida, who 'gave schools to the tenants'. The religious houses of Wales took charge of the education of boys from the local lay community, and provided for the education of their own brethren. Our evidence for these activities is often sporadic or anecdotal, for this was not necessarily a formal education. But what about their teaching methods? If they really were centres of education and scholarship, what happened to their books? Well, sadly, when the monasteries of England and Wales were closed down in the middle of the 16th century under Henry VIII, their libraries and archives were dispersed or destroyed. But even so we have the equivalent of Margam Abbey's 'library catalogue' from the 14th century, which lists well over 200 books – nearly all of which have now disappeared.

Strata Florida

PRINCES AND POLITICS

Several of Wales's religious communities were drawn into the politics of their day. Through their patrons and benefactors, and their contacts with the local lay community more generally, the monks and canons came into direct contact with the political life of medieval Wales, and on more than one occasion played an active part in it. Strata Florida in Ceredigion was founded by a Norman lord, Robert fitz Stephen, in 1164, but the following year the patronage passed to Rhys ap Gruffudd, lord of Deheubarth, who endowed it with large tracts of land around the abbey. The monks developed a strong sense of loyalty to Rhys's family. Under the year 1201 the *Brut y Tywysogion* noted that 'in that year died Gruffudd, son to the Lord Rhys, and a prince of Wales through right and inheritance, after assuming the habit of the order at Strata Florida, and there he was honourably buried.' The loyalty to the dynasty of Deheubarth included offering succour to their patrons in their final days and the solace of burial within their walls. But it was not only to their own patrons – in the case of Strata Florida the dynasty of Rhys ap Gruffudd – that the Welsh Cistercians showed loyalty. Thus, in 1238, the princes of South Wales held an assembly in the abbey, in the course of which, as the *Brut y Tywysogion* tells us, all present swore allegiance to Dafydd, son of Llywelyn ap Iorwerth and promised to recognise him as the sole heir to the principality of Gwynedd. A further example of monastic involvement in secular affairs is the attestation

45

by individual monks and canons of documents issued by Welsh princes and lords. In April 1258, for instance, the heads of Bardsey Abbey and Beddgelert and Penmon Priories acted as witnesses to negotiations between Llywelyn ap Gruffudd and Maredudd ap Rhys. This association with the Welsh princes occasionally got the Welsh monasteries into trouble with the English king. King John notoriously ravaged the buildings of Strata Florida and stabled his horses in the abbey church. Not all of Wales's religious houses, however, were loyal to the Welsh princes. Those who supported the English king, in turn, became the targets of native attacks, especially during the revolt of Owain Glyndŵr in the 15th century. The buildings of the regular canons of Talley Abbey were among those damaged during the revolt.

For many of the Welsh nobility, burial in their favourite monastery was what they desired – and received. Being buried so close to the prayers of monks was bound to have a positive impact on their souls after death. Sometimes they went even further and joined the monastery on their deathbeds – better late than never! In 1197, for example, so the *Brut y Tywysogion* tells us, 'Owein Cyfeiliog died at Strata Marcella after having assumed the habit of the order'.

FARMERS AND TRADERS

Furthermore, the religious communities of medieval Wales had a considerable impact on the economy of the country. Foremost among them were the Cistercians, so praised by Gerald of Wales for their successes of turning wasteland into civilization. Their economic activities ranged from the breeding of sheep and horses, and the running of farms and mills, to the reclaiming of land and large-scale felling of trees, by extension playing a key role in Welsh wool and, to a lesser extent, timber trade.

The economic activities of the Welsh monks, particularly the Cistercians, took them far beyond the shores of Wales. Records of 13th- and 14th-century merchants from Flanders and Italy show that the monks were exporting wool in considerable quantity – and some of it was judged to be wool of the finest quality. As well as sheep, horses were bred at Margam, Neath, Strata Florida, Cwm-hir and other monasteries, and the monks were also involved in a very wide range of agricultural and industrial activity.

SOCIAL NETWORKS

That the Welsh canons and monks also played a wider role in their society is shown by the surviving documents which testify to their involvement in activities as diverse as the care for the poor and sick, and road maintenance.

After the Dissolution of the Monasteries the sites of the houses and the monastic lands were granted to lay people. Here at Cistercian Neath, the Williams family constructed a mansion on part of the complex

'Both rich and poor are fed in the priest's court,' said Guto'r Glyn in the 15th century about the hospitality of Rhys, then abbot of Strata Florida. And this was not unusual: 'thousands,' Guto claims, 'got food from this kindly abbot' who 'gives the weak asylum.' The provision of hospitality, and of charity to the poor and needy, was a central obligation of medieval religious communities. At Carmarthen Priory, 80 poor persons were given relief, lodging was provided and hospitality was daily kept for the rich and the poor, to the great relief of the poor and the bare country'. If we were to believe the Welsh bards, then the hospitality shown by the Welsh abbots was nothing short of spectacular. 'Spices in one man's dish, oranges in another's', Tudur Aled insists that he had seen these at the abbot's table in Aberconwy Abbey! We probably ought to allow for a portion of artistic licence in the descriptions of the admiring poets who talk of the plentiful fine foods, good, French wines, mead, and much more besides, they were offered in the monasteries.

Even Gerald of Wales, often a harsh critic of religious orders, had occasional warm words of praise for them. He noted that 'the monks of the Cistercian order, who are in fact extremely abstemious, busy themselves unceasingly to provide hospitality for all and sundry, offering limitless charity to pilgrims and the needy.'

Some of the activities in which members of Wales's religious houses were involved appear to us decidedly unmonkish. We do not normally associate monks with road maintenance, and yet this is precisely what they did. On more than one occasion the English king requested the abbot and monks of Strata Florida Abbey to fulfil their duty of 'enlarging and widening the passes through the woods in divers places in Wales so that the passage for those traversing them may be safe and open.' The monks were the owners of much of the rich woodland that covered large areas of medieval Wales, and as such were responsible for making the roads safe for travellers – and not least for the king's own officials.

The monasteries and nunneries of medieval Wales all belonged to international orders with affiliations across the length and breadth of western Christendom. Their membership of these orders brought with it international contacts, which were enforced through the more or less regular visits of Welsh religious officers to houses of their order abroad, or, conversely, visits of brethren and monastic authorities to Wales. The Welsh monasteries were thereby firmly part of an international religious network, from which contacts arose an exchange of cultural influences which helped shape medieval Welsh life, culture and society.

THE MONASTIC WALES PROJECT

In order to lift the Welsh religious houses, many of whose – often exceedingly picturesque – remains still grace the Welsh landscape, from an undeserved and unjustifiable obscurity, the Monastic Wales project seeks to bring these important communities to wider attention. This project, now in its second year, seeks to provide information about Wales's medieval abbeys and priories. Its first step saw the publication of an interactive, interdisciplinary website aimed at scholars as well as students and the general public. This website, www.monasticwales.org, contains information about the monasteries and nunneries of post-Norman-Conquest Wales, including details of their foundation histories and other significant events relating to the house, and references to associated persons. As well as general information about each religious house, and a bibliography of relevant works, individual sites already include links to selected primary sources which can be accessed via the website.

6

THE MEDIEVAL CHURCH – HEAVEN OR HELL ON EARTH?

Madeleine Gray

The Catholic Church in Wales at the end of the Middle Ages was immensely powerful – but we all know that it was a power based on fear. The church held the keys of Heaven and Hell. Every parish church had a terrifying painting of the Last Judgement, usually over the chancel arch where the congregation had to look at it all through the services. You can still see one of these at Wrexham in North Wales. On the left of the painting, saved souls are being welcomed into heaven – but on the right they are pitchforked down into the eternal flames of hell.

Meanwhile, the Church itself was squalidly corrupt. Most of the parish clergy were uneducated. Worse, they broke their vows of celibacy, living openly with their mistresses. Senior clergy lived comfortably on the work of others. The whole thing was ripe for change.

Or was it? After all, all big public-sector organizations have their failings. If you went by newspaper reports, you might well conclude that the National Health Service was a disaster. But if you ask anyone who has had recent experience of medical treatment, you will probably get a very different picture. Of course, we all have our complaints about delays, and we can all think of scandals and disasters. But in general we value our NHS – it looks after us from cradle to grave.

As the medieval Church did. If we look more carefully at these terrifying pictures of the Last Judgement, we can see that they are designed to encourage as well as to condemn. In the painting at Wrexham, Jesus is wearing the red robes of a judge – but he is sitting on a rainbow, the symbol of hope. Behind him are angels holding up banners with the symbols of the crucifixion – the hammer, the nails, the spear which pierced his side. You can see the nail holes in his hands and feet and the wound in his side.

HELPING PEOPLE INTO HEAVEN

We are so used to the hellfire and damnation preaching of our chapel tradition that these paintings can still make us feel guilty and afraid. But for the medieval congregation they were also reassuring, encouraging them to think about the story of the Crucifixion and to consider how it could help them to overcome the difficulties of their daily lives. They were taught that Jesus' wounds would help them into heaven.

In Caernarfon's old parish church at Llanbeblig, up on the hill by the Roman fort, is a strange little memorial brass. It commemorates Richard Foxwist, a professional scribe from the town who died in 1500. It shows him actually on his deathbed, propped up on the pillows and clutching a painting of Jesus' five wounds – just the pierced hands and feet and a pierced heart. The inscription underneath makes it clear that Richard Foxwist is hanging on to his hope of salvation.

You even find the same pictures on fonts, the containers for holy water used to baptize babies. Sometimes these were decorated with carvings of saints and angels, but some have carvings of the symbols of the crucifixion. This looks bizarre and even gruesome to us, but the carvings were there to remind the baby's family that it was thanks to the crucifixion that the baby's sins could be washed away in baptism.

REBUILDING THE CHURCH

The evidence that the people of medieval Wales valued what the church did for them is all around us if we know where to look. Most of our medieval churches were added to in the years just before the Reformation – new towers, new porches, intricately carved wooden screens and choir stalls. Some churches were completely rebuilt in the lavish 'Perpendicular' style with elaborate fan vaulting and massive stained-glass windows. Three of the famous 'Seven Wonders of Wales' – Wrexham steeple, St Winifred's Well and Gresford bells – can still remind us of this huge enthusiasm for the church.

Gresford is now most famous for its terrible mining disaster in 1934 when 266 people were killed, but it looks nothing like the mining towns of the South Wales valleys. It is more like a traditional English village, with pretty cottages and a village green. Gresford's church was almost completely rebuilt at the end of the 15th century, with money from local traders and landowners. As well as paying for the bell tower, many of them also gave money for stained glass in the church.

The glass in the north part of the church tells the life story of Jesus' mother,

Pistyll Rhaeadr

the Virgin Mary, based on legends which didn't quite make it into the Bible. The early scenes are particularly touching. According to this legend, Mary's parents were elderly and had given up all hope of a child. Her mother (called Anna in the story) is shown in the garden, reading her prayer book. An angel appears to her and tells her that her prayers have been answered. She hurries to tell her husband, Joachim, and they are shown with their arms around each other. The next panel shows the scene after Mary's birth. Anna lies in the bed exhausted, the midwives are clustered around the baby, and Joachim has just rushed in to hold his daughter. In the foreground a servant is making some nice nourishing soup. Surely this level of detail and human feeling could not come from fear – the people of medieval Wales read these stories and made them their own, seeing in the life of Jesus and his mother a reflection of their own lives.

Holywell

But medieval religion was not just about simple and touching stories. Some of the windows have more complex and intellectual ideas behind them. Gresford church had some very powerful sponsors. The local landowner was none other than Thomas Stanley, who had married Henry VII's mother, Lady Margaret Beaufort. Thomas Stanley's troops were crucial in winning the battle of Bosworth for Henry VII and he was made Earl of Derby by his grateful stepson. He gave the money for the great east window at Gresford. The window was damaged at the Reformation (and even more damaged by later efforts at conservation) but there is enough left to allow us to guess what it looked like when it was new. At the top is a 'Tree of Jesse', a sort of pictorial family tree showing Jesus' descent from the patriarch Jesse and the kings of Israel. Below this are the three persons of the Christian Trinity – God the Father, with the triple crown of Authority; God the Son, the figure of Love; and God the Holy Spirit with the dove of Inspiration. Then there are not one but three figures of the Virgin Mary, in her relationship to each of the persons of the Trinity. The Angel Gabriel is there, to announce that Mary is going to bear God's son. Finally, there is St John the Evangelist, whose gospel in the Bible begins with the famous lines 'In the beginning was the Word, and the Word was with God, and the Word was God'.

This is all very difficult stuff! Basically, the upper part of the window is a very complicated visual discussion of the central mystery of Christianity, the God who is both 100% human and 100% divine. Below it are panels of glass illustrating the 'Te Deum', a great hymn of praise to God from the whole of creation. A church whose members could commission art of this level of complexity was surely not on the way out.

WELLS AND PILGRIMAGES

The Stanley family were also involved in the rebuilding of another of Wales's Seven Wonders, St Winifred's Well. Winifred (Gwenffrewi in Welsh) was a young woman from north-east Wales who had promised her life to God. The son of the local ruler had other ideas, and when she refused him he cut her head off. (Probably not the best way of winning her over, when you think about it, but that's energetic young men for you...) Where her head fell, a healing well sprang up. It was an important focus for pilgrimage all through the Middle Ages. At the end of the 15th century, the well and the church above it were rebuilt in the most elaborate Perpendicular style, with intricate fan vaulting and carvings showing scenes from Winifred's life.

The rebuilding seems to have been a joint project. It was probably started by Thomas Stanley's younger brother William. He was also a powerful landowner and had fought at Bosworth, but in 1495 he got mixed up in the Perkin Warbeck conspiracy and was beheaded for high treason. The project may then have been rescued by his sister-in-law, the king's mother, Lady Margaret Beaufort. She was both formidably devout and formidably intellectual (she founded two of Cambridge University's colleges). The head of the nearby abbey of Basingwerk also had a hand in the rebuilding. Finally, Cadw has tested the roof timbers of the upper chapel and has found that they date from the late 1520s – so the last work was done less than a decade before the whole shrine should have been closed down on the King's orders. (It wasn't, of course – but that is another story.)

LEADERS AND TEACHERS

But what about the clergy – were they really as bad as the government's inspectors made out? Here it is true to say that there were problems at the top. Bishops and archdeacons were senior Government officials and seldom lived in their dioceses. The Bishop of Llandaf in the early 1530s was one George de Athequa. As his name suggests, he was a foreigner – he was from Spain, and he had come to this country as Catherine of Aragon's personal chaplain. Not only could he not speak Welsh (and very few of the senior clergy could), he couldn't speak English either. He visited his diocese precisely once, in disguise, when he was on the run after Catherine's death in 1536.

Further down the hierarchy, it is also true to say that the parish priests were not as a rule particularly well educated. In other words, they had not been to university, they could not read Latin fluently and they had a very limited understanding of theology.

But how much of a problem was that? We have to remember that medieval Wales had no universities of its own. If young men were to go to university, they would have to go to Oxford or Cambridge – and they would come back with their heads full of big ideas, able to read Latin but forgetting their Welsh. Not much use in a rural parish when they had to explain the basics of the faith to a congregation of hard-working farmers or to comfort a peasant woman whose children had died.

And the clergy do seem to have been good at explaining the basics. If you read some of the poetry written at that time, you will find that a lot of it is on religious themes – and it assumes quite a high level of knowledge in its hearers. The Glamorgan poet Iorwerth Fynglwyd came from the parish of St Bride's Major near Bridgend. When he was writing about the saint of his own parish, St Brigid, he decided to link her with a more recent St Brigid who had been queen of Sweden two centuries earlier. St Brigid of Sweden wrote a series of very complex and mystical meditations on Jesus' sufferings. Iorwerth Fynglwyd referred to these meditations in his poem and clearly expected his hearers to know exactly what he was talking about.

So what about all those mistresses? To be honest, although the church wanted its priests to stay celibate, priests in outlying agricultural areas all over Europe did in fact get married. As the clergy of Gwynedd explained to Thomas Cromwell, their wives were more of a help than a hindrance in their pastoral work. It was these women who ran the household so that the church could offer charity and hospitality.

DEFENDING THE FAITH

The people of Wales were certainly prepared to defend their beliefs against Henry VIII's attacks. One of the most famous pilgrimage shrines in medieval Wales was the statue and holy well of the Virgin Mary at Penrhys, on the ridge above the Rhondda valleys. A local landowner, William Herbert of St Julian's near Newport, was ordered to destroy the shrine in the summer of 1538. You can still see his report in the National Archives in London.

At first, it looks as though it was a fairly simple job. Henry VIII's chief minister Thomas Cromwell wrote to William Herbert and told him to remove the statue as quietly and secretly as he could. When William got to Penrhys he found that the locals had gathered there – but he says in his report that he told them what they were doing wrong and took the statue away. He then says he will send it to London any day soon.

This is where the holes in his story start to appear. Why the delay? The statue was obviously hot stuff and could have sparked serious protests. Cromwell clearly expected trouble. He told William Herbert to take one of the senior church officers with him, but William couldn't find the man in Llandaf. (Diplomatic tummyache, maybe?) It took him three days to gather an armed guard, and by that time the word had obviously got out. Then he claimed to have removed the statue with no problems, but three weeks later it was still supposed to be sitting in his house outside Newport. What was he thinking of?

The obvious answer is that he had more difficulty than he was prepared to admit. There could well have been a serious fight. Why would he not want to admit this? Well, it would make him look bad. At the end of his letter, he says to Cromwell that he will be happy to

'At Penrhys is intercession in a moor of green trees.
Everyone who lives is made whole.'
(Trans. from Gwilym Tew)

Counting the rosary beads remains a Catholic observance

do anything else that the king wants – so he would not want to look as though he had made a mess of his first job. He might also have been protecting the local people. In those days, resistance to the king could result in a slow and very painful death. And finally, it is just possible that the statue was not removed at all. Three weeks would have been long enough for a replica to be made. There are plenty of other examples of statues and paintings being hidden at the Reformation and found again hundreds of years later.

But apart from these stories of early resistance, Wales seems to have accepted and even welcomed the changes of the 16th century. This is a real puzzle for Welsh historians. As far as we can see, the people of Wales were happy with their traditional Catholic faith. But there is very little evidence of resistance to change. Even in 1549, when we had to start using a prayer book in English, there were no riots (unlike Cornwall and Devon, where they had something close to civil war). And by 1588, when the Bible was finally translated into Welsh, Wales had been completely won over.

Or is that yet another myth?

THE SEVEN TRADITIONAL WONDERS OF WALES: HOW MANY HAVE YOU SEEN?

Pistyll Rhaeadr • Wrexham steeple

Mount Snowdon • Overton yew trees

St Winifred's Well • Llangollen bridge • Gresford bells.

7

WE ALL WENT TO CHAPEL, DIDN'T WE?

Madeleine Gray

The Welsh have always been a nation of chapel-goers, haven't we?

Not that we all went to the *same* chapels, of course. We all remember Ryan Davies's story about the Welsh castaway who built two chapels on his desert island. When his rescuers asked him 'Why two' he pointed to one and said 'That's the one I don't go to'.

So every mining village had its English Particular Baptists, its Welsh Strict Baptists, its English Wesleyan Methodists, its Welsh Calvinistic Methodists ... and if your village didn't have the one you wanted, you might walk five or six miles to find one. But the routine was always the same. Up early on Sunday morning, on with the best black clothes, off to Moriah, to Bethel, to Tirzah, to Shiloh, to Pisgah, for hymns in four-part harmony and a two-hour sermon. Back in the afternoon for Bible study. The old women of Rhyd-y-car near Merthyr Tydfil remembered the great Welsh Bible being placed ceremonially on the red chenille tablecloth opposite the door of their tiny houses, 'on the best side', where it could easily be seen by passers-by when the door was open. We even exported the chapels along with the language to Pennsylvania and Patagonia, where you will find chapels called Moriah, Bethel and Tirzah.

But the problem is that it wasn't always like that.

Standing room only in chapel: an image of Sundays past

For over a millennium before the Reformation, Wales was part of the universal Catholic Church. Even if you are a bit sceptical about the story of the first Welsh martyrs Julius and Aaron and their sticky end in the Caerleon amphitheatre, Christianity came to Wales as part of the Roman empire. The first Christian churches were in Roman towns like Caerwent. From there, Christianity spread slowly out into the countryside, helped by the decline of town life as the Roman empire gradually disintegrated.

But what about the Age of the Saints? Surely the Celtic church of Dewi, Padarn and Teilo was independent, standing out against the control of the Pope in Rome? Well, maybe...

CELTS AND ROMANS

The church in Wales certainly had its differences with Rome. Church leaders shaved their heads differently; they used a different formula for calculating the date of Easter, producing the sort of chaos you get today when your children's schools have different half-terms. The Northumbrian monk-historian Bede (who was an Anglo-Saxon and didn't like the Welsh) accused us of not doing baptism properly, but he never said what we were actually doing wrong. More significantly, the Welsh church may have adopted some of the ideas of the Irish church on the key doctrine of penance. In the early Roman church, breaking the rules meant public confession and penance, sitting separately in the church and wearing sackcloth and ashes. This survived into the later Middle Ages, and the Easter service for the reconciliation of penitents is one of the most moving rites in the medieval liturgy. But in the early church it really was 'two strikes and you're out' – break the rules again and you were permanently excluded. It was the Irish who came up with the idea of private confession to a priest, followed by a penance which you could also do privately – and you could be forgiven again and again.

For all these differences, though, the Welsh church was always part of the international Catholic Church. The idea of an independent 'Celtic' church which defied the authority of the Pope in Rome was largely an invention of Welsh historians after the Reformation. If we are honest, we have to admit that most historians have some sort of an agenda. In the case of the Welsh historians of the 16th century, they wanted to convince the people of Wales that the Reformation was simply reclaiming the ideas of the early Welsh saints.

The early Welsh saints wouldn't have seen it that way, though. The stories of their lives proudly record their pilgrimages to Rome and their meetings with the Pope. The first version of the life of St Gwenffrewi (or Winifred) tells how she went to Rome to renew her vows, brought back St Benedict's idea of supportive monastic communities, summoned a general meeting of the British church to advocate the new ideas and founded a model community of her own. (This episode was written out of later versions of the story – possibly because male Benedictine monks didn't like the idea of a woman as their role model.)

Saint Winifred and Saint Beuno

MONKS AND SAINTS

After the Norman conquest, the medieval church in Wales was very much part of an international organization. The archetypal Welsh monk was a Cistercian, and the Cistercians were a centralized order with houses from Spain to Poland. Admittedly, the Cistercians went native pretty quickly in Wales. They provided the Welsh kings with advisers and a secretariat. They wrote to the Pope on behalf of Llywelyn ap Gruffudd, and the abbot of Llantarnam died on the battlefield of Usk with Owain Glyndŵr's troops. But for all that, the Cistercians in Wales were part of a multi-national conglomerate and emphatically Catholic.

For ordinary Welsh people, too, the Catholic Church underpinned their everyday lives and their most powerful aspirations. We still had the Welsh saints but we also had the saints of the international tradition – Catherine of Alexandria, Margaret of Antioch, and above all the Virgin Mary herself. Medieval Wales was notable for its devotion to the Virgin Mary. As God's own mother, she was the most powerful of saints and could intercede for you at the Last Judgement. At Llanelian near Colwyn Bay there is a painting of her putting her rosary beads on the scales of judgement to weigh it down on the side of salvation. Another of the most popular saints, to judge from the number of wall paintings of him which survive, was St Christopher. He is now best known as the patron of travellers, but in the Middle Ages he was the saint who could protect you from an evil death. Not that he could keep you from dying – that was not important! But he could make sure that you died a good death, with time to repent and confess your sins, be absolved by a priest and receive the last rites, the anointing with holy oil that would speed you on your way. As well as wall paintings, he was carved on tombs. If you look carefully at the tomb of Sir Christopher Matthew in the Lady Chapel of Llandaff Cathedral, you will see that his effigy has a little St Christopher medallion on its breast – a permanent prayer to the saint to look after him.

PACKAGE TOURS AND PILGRIMAGES

Medieval people didn't have package holidays but they did have pilgrimages. You went on a pilgrimage to pray for healing (for yourself or your loved ones), to do penance for your sins or as an act of devotion, but it was also fun and a break from routine. Pilgrimage could be local, an afternoon's walk to a nearby shrine, but plenty of Welsh people went much further afield – even as far as what Lewys Glyn Cothi called the '*tair ffynnon gwynion i'r drugaredd*' (the Three Blessed Fountains of Mercy): Rome, Santiago and the Holy Land. In St Mary's Church, Swansea, you can still see the tombstone of Sir Hugh Johnys of Landimore. It records with pride that he was dubbed a knight of the Holy Sepulchre when he was in Jerusalem in 1441. Many of the Welsh bards went on pilgrimage to Rome. Huw Cae Llwyd took his young son with him, and they were amazed by the city's treasures. If you wanted to count the relics there, he said, you might just as well try to count the pebbles of the sea. Perhaps the most popular overseas attraction for Welsh pilgrims, though, was the shrine of St James at Compostela in northern Spain. Transport was easier – you could travel with the returned empties from the wine trade – but it was still a terrifying journey, beset by storms and pirates.

These pilgrimages overseas made Wales part of the international Catholic world, but for ordinary peasants and labourers there were literally hundreds of local shrines to choose from. Many of them were linked to holy wells. There were famous wells like Penrhys and Holywell which attracted pilgrims in their thousands, and wells dedicated to otherwise unknown saints like St Ceinwen's Well on Anglesey. Most people went to these wells for healing, but they could also be used to foretell the future and even to curse your enemies. This, you could say, is the dark side of the Welsh identity. On the one hand, the chapel and the William Morgan Bible; on the other hand, 'Celtic' religion, strange rituals in dark places. Some of the wells may even go back to pre-Christian times. The story of St Winifred's well at Holywell has disturbing echoes of Celtic head cults. Winifred was a devout young woman. Her head was cut off by a disappointed suitor but her mentor St Beuno healed her (and killed the young man). Where her head fell to the ground, a powerful spring gushed out, and the moss which grew there was stained as if by blood. At nearby Tremeirchion, Beuno's own well flows through the mouth of a stone head. Of course, we cannot prove any of this: all we know is that these wells were used in the Middle Ages. In many cases they even survived the Reformation, to the horror of Protestant ministers.

The Catholic Church even underpinned the economic life of medieval Welsh towns. We now have a South Wales Chamber of Commerce, but in the 15th century Cardiff's tradespeople had the Guilds of Holy Trinity and St Mary. They represented the interests of the town's leading craftspeople, but they also organised religious services and arranged for funerals and prayers for their members. You can still see the seal of the Trinity guild, a sort of brandmark with which the guild would have authenticated its documents, in the National Museum in Cathays Park. It has a tiny, intricately detailed depiction of the Trinity as a

There being not only Churches and Chapels but springs and fountains dedicated to those saints, they do at certain times go and bathe themselves in them, and sometimes leave some small oblations behind them, for the Benefit they have or hope to have thereby

Erasmus Saunders, *A View of the State of Religion in the Diocese of St David's*, 1721

61

medieval Catholic would have envisaged it. God the Father sits on his throne, cradling the crucified Christ in his arms, while the dove of the Holy Spirit hovers above. This is all very reminiscent of the medieval Italian merchant bank which put God on the list of shareholders (his dividend was given to the poor).

BRINGING COLOUR INTO EVERYDAY LIFE

As anyone who has seen the rebuilt St Teilo's Church at the National History Museum in St Fagan's will know, even the simplest village churches were a riot of colour, light and music. Stories from the Bible were depicted in crude and vivid wall paintings, saints and apostles were brightly painted on screens and as statues. The air would have been thick with incense and candle smoke. There would have been music, too: the hypnotic Gregorian chant, simple polyphony, perhaps improvised as the Welsh later improvised *penillion*. There may even have been a miniature organ (something about the same size as a chapel harmonium) to accompany the singing. Wealthier churches had stained glass, and the sunlight would have glowed through pictures of saints and angels.

The east window of the church at Llandyrnog in the Vale of Clwyd gives us an amazing insight into the whole range of medieval Catholic religion in Wales. It is dominated by the central figure of Christ on the cross. Blood streams from his wounds. The blood becomes red banners leading to the seven sacraments of the Catholic church – baptism, confirmation, penance, Communion, marriage, ordination and the last rites. The glass panel depicting Marriage is particularly touching. A happy young couple in their best clothes are surrounded by their friends. The priest has just joined their hands together. A red streamer points directly at the bride's heart: Jesus' suffering is actually blessing her love for the young man and their marriage.

Around these central scenes are fragments of other pictures. Some of the Apostles are holding scrolls with verses from the Apostles' Creed, the basic Christian statement of belief. On one side are two Welsh bishop-saints, David and Asaph. (Interestingly, David is shown not as an ordinary bishop but as an archbishop with a cross-staff and the ceremonial robe called the *pallium* – and this was 450 years before Wales officially gained its own archbishop.) On the other side are the most famous of the Welsh female saints, Gwenffrewi; St Catherine, the martyred princess from Alexandria; St Frideswide, who was a hermit near Oxford and became the patron saint of Oxford University – what is she doing here? – and St Marcella, Tyrnog's sister and a local hermit. At the top are a couple of episodes from the life of the Virgin Mary. In one, she is kneeling at a prayer desk when the angel appears to her to tell her she will be the mother of God's son. Above this is the end of the story: she has been taken bodily up to Heaven and is being crowned by Jesus.

The St Teilo's Project has really made us rethink our ideas on what it is to be Welsh. Long before the days of Shiloh, Tirzah and Moriah, we had Llan Deilo, Llan Badarn, Llan Ddewi, the churches of the Catholic saints. So how did Wales come to be that nation of chapel-goers? How was it possible for a millennium of tradition to be swept away? Of course, the late medieval Catholic church in Wales was powerful; but it was also corrupt, ruling by fear of hellfire and damnation. Its priests were ignorant, slovenly, living in open sin with their mistresses. By 1530 people were desperate for change.

Or is that another myth?

St Teilo's Church

8

WAS THE REFORMATION WELCOMED IN WALES?

Katharine Olson

There is an idea that unlike places such as Yorkshire, where the new Protestant faith provoked defiance and rebellion, the Welsh welcomed the Protestant Reformation with open arms. To people in Wales as elsewhere, then, the Protestant Reformation was a vast improvement on the excesses and corruption of the medieval Catholic Church and its disastrous clergy. They understood little of its teachings, were apathetic, and believed in superstitious nonsense instead. They were frightened into religion by talk of hellfire and damnation. Protestantism meant progress. The Reformation experienced great success in Wales, and brought an immediate end to the medieval church and all its problems and bad practices. It brought with it much-needed improvements, modernization, and the Welsh-language Bible. By the time this was printed in 1588, the Reformation had already been achieved in Wales. It was inevitable.

Or was it? Is the idea of a quick, easy, popular Reformation in Wales just another myth?

Protestantism was in fact not speedily welcomed by everyone in Wales. Most initially had no wish for change, and the medieval Catholic Church did not deserve all the bad press it has received. Some came to embrace the Church of England for reasons of faith, others for expediency. Others remained confused, and simply did not understand the changes. Many in Wales came to accept the new church over a long time; but equally, others never did, or wished to reform it. It had an uncertain future.

WALES AND THE REFORMATION: CHANGES

The English Reformation was begun by Henry VIII, who split with Rome so he could divorce the first of his six wives – Katherine of Aragon – and marry the captivating Anne Boleyn instead. But his actions set into motion a number of important changes in Wales. This was an uncertain and confusing time, as his successors alternately continued, reversed and then reinstated Protestant religious reforms – it is not for nothing that historians talk of a *series* of reformations during this period.

True, there were no armed uprisings in Wales in response to this turmoil. But this did not mean that the Welsh were unmoved. It may not have been in their best interest to resist the changes through rebelling, but other means of showing dissent existed.

The first targets of Henry's changes were the Welsh abbeys and friaries; their lands were confiscated and their monks ejected. But by 1538, the images that the Welsh had prayed to in their parish churches and visited on pilgrimage for centuries were called 'superstitious' and 'idolatry', and were to be removed and destroyed. In 1548, it was decided that images in stained-glass windows, stone, and wood, which were such a part of Catholic devotion, also had to go.

The constable of Rhiwabon (Denbighshire), Ieuan ap William ap Dafydd, witnessed these changes at his local parish church first-hand. He wrote of how Henry VIII had the images pulled down, dissolved the monasteries, and 'took their life'. Just ten years later, under Henry VIII's son, Edward VI, a pulpit was built in Rhiwabon to enable the better preaching of sermons, and soon after the old altar was taken down.

Reformation changes, however, were not instantaneous. The Welsh were accused of reacting unenthusiastically to the new religion. But just *how* fast these changes occurred and *how* effective they were in deciding people's religious beliefs and practices depended largely on local circumstances, people, and authorities.

For example, some images, hidden away for years, survived both the destruction of the Reformation and the Civil War a century later. The beautiful Jesse window at Llanrhaeadr-yng-Nghinmeirch (Denbighshire) is alleged to have survived thanks to parishioners there, who disassembled it and hid it in the vast parish chest. In Mochdre (Montgomeryshire), a figure of Christ and another possibly of the Virgin Mary were found in 1867, concealed under the wall-plate of the church there; and in Mold, a peculiar image was discovered in 1768 in the tower wall. The paintings found hidden beneath centuries of paint in St Teilo's church (Pontarddulais, now at St Fagan's) have been recreated in stunning detail, allowing visitors today to see what the walls of a medieval church may have looked like. It is possible that other pre-Reformation paintings and images may exist, buried under layers of whitewash or otherwise hidden from view.

PILGRIMAGES AND HOLY WELLS

Nevertheless, many Catholic beliefs and practices persisted despite the changes. The authorities were infuriated by the continued popularity of pilgrimages to shrines and holy wells in Wales. Thomas Cromwell's right-hand man, the Protestant Dr Ellis Price of Plas Iolyn, was responsible for overseeing many royal commands in North Wales. In 1538, he visited the popular shrine of Llandderfel (Meirionnydd) on the feast day of Derfel Gadarn, its patron saint. His report was scathing: hundreds of pilgrims had come on pilgrimage to Llandderfel with cows, oxen, horses, and money. They intended to give these as offerings to the saint, whose wooden statue there was reputed to work all sorts of miracles, including fetching people's souls out of hell. He promptly had the statue removed and burnt.

Yet pilgrimages continued despite these strong-arm tactics. More than fifty years later, Price reported to the government about events in Clynnog Fawr (Caernarfonshire). People still observed the feast day of St Beuno; they sacrificed bulls in Beuno's honour, and gave other offerings to him as well, thinking him the most powerful of all the saints, he claimed. In fact, people continued to come from far and wide to ask for Beuno's help with their sick livestock and other concerns for many years afterward. Beuno's well was also thought to have special powers to cure sickness.

Certainly, Protestant bishops in many areas of Wales were not happy with the slow responses of the people to reforms. The bishop of Bangor spoke in 1567 of how he saw the same old images and altars in churches, and various 'lewd and indecent' celebrations of traditional feast days. He complained too that the people still lit candles for saints and their relics, and carried around Catholic rosaries. In South Wales, the bishop of St Davids expressed concern in 1577 that people still defended Catholicism, and followed 'superstition and idolatry', went on pilgrimages, and concealed forbidden images, altars, and other items.

But this discouragement did not always lead to abandonment. Devotions to the saints and pilgrimages to their holy places and wells continued into the eighteenth century and beyond in Wales at places like Holywell, where miracles were still proclaimed. Interest in stories about the saints continued, and took their place in Welsh folk culture. The Catholic carol 'Myn Mair', sung to the Virgin Mary, probably dates from the 1500s or earlier. This carol, however, was collected in the 1930s from a Cardiganshire teacher, Myra Evans, whose mother had taught it to her: a reminder of the long life of many Welsh Catholic traditions.

'O Mother of Jesus, most beautiful of all women in the world,
Virgin Queen of all the heavens,
Lovely lily of the valley, praiseworthy rose of heaven,
Intercede powerfully for the soul of my friend.
In Mary's name.'

Trans. From *Myn Mair*

PRINT, EDUCATION, AND THE CLERGY

Protestantism has been called the 'religion of the book.' Having the Bible and other religious works available for people in English to use and study was central to its success in England. But if the Welsh could not understand or read English, they would not be persuaded by Protestant ideas. From 1549, all worship in Wales was to be in English, but most people in Wales *only* spoke Welsh. In 1551 when the Protestant Bishop Ferrar preached in English in Abergwili near Carmarthen, only three or four parishioners out of about 140 understood him.

So did the 1588 Welsh Bible signal Welsh Protestantism's ultimate victory? By itself, no. But language *was* a central issue for the Protestants in Wales. It was for this reason that they lobbied to get Parliament to pass an Act in 1563 to remedy the language situation. They were ultimately successful: Welsh could now be used for worship too. Welsh churches were required to have English *and* Welsh versions of the Bible and Book of Common Prayer. But while Welsh versions of the Book of Common Prayer and New Testament were published in 1567, people had to wait much longer for a full Bible in Welsh.

The 1588 Welsh Bible of William Morgan certainly played a vital part in the survival of the Welsh language. But it *in itself* was not the saving grace of the Protestant Reformation. It was meant to be read in church, not to be taken home. It arrived slowly at churches in some cases, and was too expensive for most people to buy and read privately. In fact, a more affordable Welsh Bible did not get published until 1630, when the 'little bible' sold for five shillings.

Bishop William Morgan

So the mere existence of the 1588 Bible only went so far. It was up to people in Wales to to take advantage of it by actively using and reading it. Yet, above and beyond its steep price, these imperatives presented problems as well. The majority of the population would be illiterate for a century and more to come.

Moreover, most of the clergy were not qualified enough to put the Bible to good use or preach. The shortage of qualified Anglican clergy was no trivial issue: the scale of the problem was immense. In 1561, shortly after Elizabeth I

I find....that ignorance continues many in the dregs of superstition.....for the most part the priests are too old, they say, now to be put to school. Upon this inability to teach God's word....I have found since I came to the country images and altars standing in churches undefaced, lewd and indecent vigils and watches observed, much pilgrimage-going, many candles set up in honour of saints, some relics yet carried about, and all the county full of beads and knots [rosaries].

Nicholas Robinson,
Bishop of Bangor, 1567

came to the throne, in the whole diocese of Bangor only two men were able to preach, and only five in the dioceses of St Asaph and Llandaf. It was only in the 1590s that a handful of competent preachers had begun to come along, but many of these could only preach in English. The problem only improved slowly. Even in 1595 the vicar of Llanddeiniolen complained that there were *still* no capable priests; they were lazy, like dogs who could not bark, or bells that could not ring.

The Anglican Church in Wales in the 16th and 17th centuries also had another problem: it was quite poor. The Welsh clergy did not earn as much as others; many held multiple appointments to get by. Obviously, they could not be everywhere at once, so some parishes got neglected, or farmed out to little-qualified replacements. Sometimes parishes went without regular services at all. Nevertheless, even a reasonable income did not guarantee qualified clergy, as the complaints of people in Churchstoke (Montgomeryshire) demonstrate: all they got were 'unlearned, poor, bare, and needy fellows'. The poverty of the Welsh church lingered for many years.

CATHOLIC DISSENT IN WALES

Welsh Catholicism was actually the first Nonconformism. Catholics opposed the new Anglican Church in different ways, from failing to attend services, circulating Catholic books, hiding fugitive priests, and even plotting to overthrow the government.

But those families who remained Catholics defied the Church of England and government policy at their own risk. With the Protestant Elizabeth I on the throne, those who refused to attend church services became known as recusants, and faced a variety of penalties. By 1581, merely being a recusant could potentially cost you up to £20 a month (a small fortune today), and by 1593, recusants could not go more than five miles from their houses.

The failure of Guy Fawkes's Gunpowder Plot to blow up Parliament in 1605 was bad news for Welsh recusants. The government decided to crack down on them even more, worried that another Catholic plot might just succeed. Now convicted recusants had to take Anglican communion at least once a year; if not, they paid crippling fines and could lose all their property. Catholics were also forbidden from holding lands, office, and entering the professions.

The conspirators of the Gunpowder Plot

Other punitive laws followed through the 17th century; it was not until 1829 that Catholics could sit in Parliament or hold office again.

However, prominent recusant families remained scattered throughout Wales. They included the Pughs of Penrhyn Creuddyn, the Morgans of Llantarnam, the earls of Worcester at Raglan, the Herberts of Powis Castle, the Mostyns of Talacre, the Edwardses of Plas Newydd, the Owens of Plas Du, and the Turbervilles in the Vale of Glamorgan.

Yet those who clung to the Catholic faith also included spinsters, widows, bakers, weavers, labourers, servants, farmers, and many others. Women were very important to the recusant cause in Wales, as in England. Often a wife stayed at home while her husband kept up appearances by attending Anglican services. Some people outwardly conformed to avoid stiff fines, but secretly remained Catholic.

The Catholic cause in Wales was supported by the circulation of Welsh books as well. Indeed, the first Welsh book of any kind to be printed on Welsh soil was a Catholic book called *Y Drych Cristianogawl* ('The Christian Mirror'), probably written by the priest Robert Gwyn (d.1592/1604?) of Llanarmon (Llŷn), and was secretly printed near Llandudno, in a cave located on the Little Orme's Head, in 1586/7.

Like the undercover priest Robert Gwyn, other Welshmen took a more active and extreme line to combat the Anglican establishment. In 1581, it was made treason to convert to Catholicism, or to try to convert someone else to it; further measures followed, and the penalty for being caught was often death. Still, Catholic priests, some of them missionaries raised in Wales but trained on the continent, defied the law. It was a perilous life, and some Welsh homes still have priest holes, where these men hid from the authorities. A number of Welsh Catholics (mostly priests) were executed in the 16th and 17th centuries, some of whom have been canonized, like St Richard Gwyn (d.1584), a schoolmaster martyred in Wrexham, and St David Lewis (d.1679), martyred in Usk.

2010 marked the 400th anniversary of the martyrdom of one of these men, St John Roberts. He was born in Trawsfynydd in c1576/7, and came from a well-connected Meirionnydd family. But he converted to Catholicism, and became a Benedictine priest in Spain, taking the name of Juan de Mervinia (John of Meirionnydd). Despite the dangers, he returned to England and ministered to the poor and sick in London. He was arrested, and martyred on December 10, 1610, at Tyburn, where he was hanged, drawn, and quartered. In 1970, he was canonized. In 2010, a mass was held for him at Cymer Abbey (near Dolgellau), and at another service to mark the anniversary of his martyrdom in London, Welsh was officially spoken for the first time at Westminster Cathedral.

PROTESTANT DISSENT

The authorities may have seen the Catholic recusants as the main threat to the Church of England at this time, but they were not always alone in their Nonconformism and dissent. With time, other Protestant groups who disagreed with the established church grew up in Wales.

Perhaps the most important of these for the period up to 1660 in Wales were the Puritans, or 'the godly', as they called themselves. Unhappy with the Anglican Church, they felt that the reformation of religion had not gone far enough, and wanted to cleanse it of what they saw as evil practices and beliefs that still smacked of Catholicism. They wanted everyone to live a godly and disciplined life, based around the Bible's teachings. Puritanism had gained a small foothold in Wales by the late 1500s.

John Penry (d.1593) of Breconshire was perhaps one of Wales's most celebrated early Puritans, and its most famous Protestant martyr. Trained at Cambridge, he embraced radical Puritan ideas, and was deeply unhappy with the state of the church in Wales and its 'swarms of ungodly ministers'. He published a number of attacks on it that got him into trouble with the authorities. He was condemned to death in London and martyred in 1593.

By the 1630s, Puritanism was gaining strength in Wales, especially in the market towns of the south and north east – trading centres where new ideas spread, and more people understood English. They played a crucial part in the English Civil War (1642–1651), and the government of Oliver Cromwell (1559–1658). But their vision of a godly state did not last, and most of Wales supported the restoration of the monarchy in 1660.

In 1660, however, the church in Wales still had its problems. It remained plagued by poverty and neglect, and clergy who were habitually absent. But amidst the Civil War and its aftermath, new dissenting Protestant groups in Wales were becoming a force to be reckoned with. By 1660, both the Welsh Baptists and the Quakers had come to prominence – but theirs is another story.

> We have preaching. How often? Quarterly. It is not so. For that one parish where there is one ordinary quarter sermon, we have twenty that have none.
>
> John Penry, *Three Treatises Concerning Wales*, 1587

TIMELINE

1533-1534:	Henry VIII splits with Rome
1553:	Mary Tudor, Henry's daughter, becomes Queen; she works to restore Catholicism
1558:	Elizabeth I, a Protestant, takes the throne after Mary's death
1593:	John Penry, a Welsh Puritan, is martyred in London
1610:	St John Roberts, a Welsh Benedictine priest, is martyred at Tyburn
1630s:	Substantial growth of Puritanism in Wales
1640s:	Growth of the Baptists in Wales
1650s:	Growth of the Quakers in Wales

Llyn y Fan Fach

9

WAS WALES A MEDICAL BACKWATER?

Alun Withey

Ask most people to name even one thing about Welsh medical history and they will probably struggle. I was once asked by an academic colleague what my area of research was. When I replied that I study the medical history of Stuart Wales, he looked puzzled, frowned and said 'I didn't know there was one'! But my bewildered colleague had a point; in the wider medical history of the 17th and 18th centuries, Wales is largely anonymous. Anonymous, that is, except for the wealth of books, articles and websites about magic, cunning folk and the 'legendary' Physicians of Myddfai. Put these shadowy figures into a well-known internet search engine and your screen will light up with literally thousands of hits from scholarly articles to homeopathic healing sites. But what do we in Wales *really* know of the medical history of our own land three hundred or so years ago? From whom, for instance, did you seek advice, treatment or buy medicines? Was it really all magic and folklore or is there another story waiting to be told?

The legend of *Meddygon Myddfai* ('the Physicians of Myddfai') looms large in Welsh medical history. The first recorded physician connected to the legend is Rhiwallon, reputed son of the farmer and lake fairy of legend. Rhiwallon was the court physician to 'Rhys Grug' (Rhys the hoarse/stammerer), a local Carmarthenshire lord who died in 1233. By the 14th century, stories about a renowned family of physicians in Myddfai were apparently widespread and, also around this time, the first of several manuscript collections of the treatments and health rules of Meddygon Myddfai were assembled. In these collections were large numbers of remedies for a wide variety of ailments from common coughs and colds to sleeping potions, as well as other useful information

'If one were to ask for what the Welsh were noted as a nation, we [would] not answer contributions to the practice of medicine'.

Eminent physician and antiquarian David Fraser-Harris, 1923.

73

such as lucky and unlucky days in the year. These collections survive and give an enormously important insight into Medieval Welsh herbal medicine. The line of Myddfai physicians continued down the centuries, the last who actually practised medicine generally accepted to be one David Jones who died in 1739.

THE (BRIEF) LEGEND OF MEDDYGON MYDDFAI:

One day, a man was grazing his cattle near Llyn y Fan Fach when he spotted a beautiful maiden on the water. He reached out for her, offering bread, but she refused. The next day he returned and was again refused. On the third day, she accepted his bread and consented to marry him on the condition that he did not strike her three blows without cause. If he did, she would disappear forever. The couple married and had three sons but, over the years, he indeed struck her accidentally three times. The maiden, as forewarned, returned to the lake leaving him heartbroken. Their sons went to the lake to search for her and, after some days, she appeared to their eldest, Rhiwallon, giving him a bag of medical preparations, and told him that he and his descendants would become great healers. After showing him where to find healing plants in Myddfai, she returned finally to the lake.

There was certainly a strong vernacular Welsh tradition of magical healing. Beliefs in what might rather clumsily be termed 'folklore' had much to do with lively Welsh traditions of storytelling. Pre-industrial life in small communities meant time spent in close proximity to others and a myriad of opportunities to gossip and recount tales to friends and neighbours. Local festivals and gatherings were important outlets for popular myths and legends and some communities even had their own storytellers to keep the old traditions alive. Medical knowledge formed an important part of this verbal world and medical remedies were passed on through families and communities. At a time when even a cold could kill, sharing knowledge was logical. Also, although officially Protestant, the Welsh seemed particularly reluctant to relinquish pre-Reformation beliefs and practices such as saints' days and festivals. Beliefs in magic, spirits and the power of the *Dyn Hysbys* ('cunning man') persisted.

PILLS, POTIONS AND CHARMS

Belief in the healing powers of charms, rituals and symbols were widespread. Pins or buttons might be dropped into wells as an offering, while rags dipped into the waters of healing wells were left on trees as offerings to benevolent spirits. Evidence of charms against witches or protections against the 'evil eye' can be found all over Wales. Healing rituals, such as specific prayers or charms, were often strongly connected to religious imagery. One popular Welsh charm for toothache ran something like this:

Jesus came to Peter as he stood at the gate of Jerusalem and said unto him: 'What doest thou here?' Peter answered and said unto Jesus, 'Lord, my teeth do ache'. Jesus answered and said unto Peter, 'that whosoever carry these words in memory with them, or near them, shall never have the tooth ache any more.

Charms such as this might be obtained from the local *Dyn Hysbys* who also undertook to heal a range of ailments with his own special arsenal of magically-invested ingredients and spells.

All sorts of animal, mineral and plant products could have potential healing powers. The 'snake-stone' or 'adder-stone' was a polished river pebble resembling a snake's eye which was used to treat eye complaints. Impaling a snail onto a pin and letting the liquid drop into the eye was also believed to refresh sore eyes. One Myddfai remedy for gangrene involved beating a black toad until it became so furious that it swelled and died, baking it to a powder in a large earthenware vessel, then applying it to the wound. Although perhaps weird to modern eyes, such remedies were a normal part of medical lore. Apart from frogs, any number of other substances from animal dung to human breast milk or even powder made from dead bodies (known as 'mummy'!) could find their way into popular remedies.

Remedies could be vague – one showing how to discern a skin condition known as 'King's Evil' suggested holding an earthworm to the 'aggrieved place' to see if the worm died. It neglected to say for how long! They were often painful. A cure for constipation in one Welsh source involved squatting over a large bucket of boiling milk 'for as long as the party can bear it'. They could also be difficult to manufacture. 'Oil of Swallows' required the collection of twenty or more live swallows, and baking them in a pot with a number of other ingredients. The logistics of collecting the swallows, together with the problems of getting twenty of them into one pot alive is, unfortunately, not recorded.

But, although traditional medicine is undoubtedly important, the problem with emphasising 'folklore' in general is that it tends to evoke a certain type of imagery. This risks making 17th-century Wales look rather like a quaint little enclave, tucked away on the edge of Britain, and cut off from the outside world. Do we really want to believe that, while the literati of London were grappling with the mysteries of science and the cosmos, the Welsh were all running around in smocks bewitching each other's cattle? It's time to redress the balance and, to truly find 'Welsh medicine', we must look beyond Wales. This might seem disappointing, if not even a little strange, but we need to understand the extent to which it was part of a much bigger picture. Apparently backward, remote and insular, little Wales was actually linked in to networks of medical knowledge and practice that extended not only across the borders into England, but spanned oceans and continents.

WALES IN THE 'MEDICAL MARKETPLACE'

At first glance, 17th-century Wales certainly doesn't much resemble a medical hub. In Britain, the official centre for most things medical was London, where the royal colleges of surgeons and physicians were located. Theoretically, practising medicine required an official licence, either from a bishop of the local diocese, by graduation from Oxford or Cambridge or from one of the royal colleges. Unlike London, Glasgow, Edinburgh and Dublin, Wales had no royal colleges and no training hospitals, meaning that those wishing to obtain a medical degree were forced to leave and many never returned. With no Welsh medical profession, and no printing press on Welsh soil until 1718, there was seemingly little opportunity for Welsh doctors to enter debates or publish volumes of medical theory or remedies. Robert Recorde of Tenby was one who achieved notoriety in the 16th century with books such as *A Treatise of Urine*, but wrote from England and in English. The vast majority of Welsh people were illiterate, and spoke only Welsh anyway. In fact, the first Welsh-language medical text wasn't actually printed until 1732, some 150 years after the first English-language one.

Robert Recorde

However, there is much evidence to show that many literate Welsh people bought English-language medical books and were keen to keep up with the latest developments. The Monmouthshire yeoman-farmer John Gwin owned several English medical books, probably purchased from Bristol which he visited regularly. Many others compiled their own collections of remedies and there is much evidence of individual recipes copied directly from English books. In 1747, John Morgan of Palleg near Swansea copied passages from an English book entitled *Physical Observations*, while Humffrey Owen, a blacksmith, copied recipes from a volume by a Swiss doctor, entitled *Eighteen Books of the Secrets of Art and Nature* which included a remedy to improve memory involving the use of a (still-beating) lapwing's heart! By the end of the

17th century too, cheap Welsh-language almanacs were becoming available, which gave a range of information from general news to medical remedies and also places to buy from in London.

Welsh towns were also a potentially lucrative target for medical quacks and pedlars. In North Wales, there are even references to the presence of learned Italian physicians selling their wares to eager Welsh crowds. Unfortunately, an over-excited Wrexham crowd proved too much for an 'Italian Mountebank' called Giovanni in 1663, when a scuffle broke out on the stage and his servant was killed, perhaps by a disgruntled customer. But the presence of such people shows that Wales was open for business. Actually, large numbers of itinerant traders from different parts of Britain and Europe criss-crossed Wales selling many types of goods, doubtless including medicines and ingredients for remedies. Travelling 'vagabonds', such as the one who offered to cure Robert Bulkeley's sore tooth in Dronwy, Anglesey, in 1632, claimed to fix all manner of ailments, in Bulkeley's case taking his money but leaving him with the toothache!

Rather than just herbal medicines and charms, a range of medical goods and ready-made remedies could be purchased. The apothecary was the 17th-century's dispensing chemist, and most Welsh towns and even villages would have had one. From surviving shop inventories, it is clear that Welsh apothecaries often stocked a wide variety of goods. Visitors to the shop of Benjamin Price in Haverfordwest around 1650 would have been greeted by shelves full of gallipots, jars, bottles, plasters and razors. In John Bell's Denbighshire shop were a range of painted majolica drug jars containing compound medicines, jars and vials of expensive oils, enough to rival London apothecaries. Many Welsh apothecaries maintained accounts with their London counterparts, ordering medicines directly and then selling them on, while some Welsh gentry also held personal accounts with London apothecaries, cutting out the middle man. Advertisements for medicines in London often included references to Welsh agents from whom their wares could be purchased, suggesting again that the Welsh were part of this busy, metropolitan market.

Several records also suggest that some apothecaries in Wales even sold the latest types of medicines, such as new 'chemical' medicines popular around the middle of the 17th century. These types of shops were mainly limited to larger towns, but even non-medical retailers in small villages sold a surprising range of medical goods. The shop of Jane Lewis of Llanblethian in Glamorgan stocked everything from foodstuffs to millinery, soap, candles and tobacco. But she also sold a number of foreign spices which could be used in medical remedies, such as 'Jamaica Pepper', turmeric and ginger. Others, such as

John Thomas of Llandaf, sold cinnamon and nutmeg alongside medicines like the foul-tasting syrup of buckthorn. Exotic spices became increasingly popular in the 17th century, and highlight the fact that Welsh ports traded along a number of routes, both national and international. The close proximity of large English ports such as Bristol also brought much opportunity for imports. But the crucial point here is that, even in this very small way, Jane Lewis and John Thomas played their part in a global market which linked the spice islands of Asia, with small Welsh village shops.

MYDDFAI MYTH OR REALITY?

Were 'cunning folk' and wizards, therefore, the only Welsh medical practitioners? No. In 17th-century Wales, as elsewhere, 'doctors' were everywhere; it's just a case of knowing where to look. Relatively few Welsh doctors bothered to obtain an official licence, probably as it simply wasn't necessary, being so far from London. Still, many referred to themselves as 'doctor' and were known as such. Wills in the National Library of Wales contain scores of records for those with titles such as 'doctor', 'surgeon', 'physitian', 'barber-surgeon' and so on, with little evidence to suggest that they possessed formal qualifications.

SOME REMEDIES OF THE MYDDFAI PHYSICIANS

Diseased Eyelids – Remedy for a dry scurvy condition of the eye(lids).
Take the juice of a strawberry, a hen's fat and May butter. Pound them well together and keep in a horn (box). When going to bed anoint (about) thin eyes and eyelids well, and they will be cured.

Warts to Remove
Whosoever would remove warts, let him apply daisy bruised in dog's urine thereto, and they will all disappear.

Reptiles in the stomach – To expel them
If a snake should enter a person's mouth, or there should be any other living reptile in him, let him take wild camomile (in powder) in wine, till it is thickened, and drink the same as it will relieve him of them.

For the toothache
Take shepherd's purse and pound it into a mass, then apply to the tooth.

From *Welsh Traditions and Traits*, Chris Stephens (Gomer, 2007)

In fact, we shouldn't even draw a distinction between types of practitioners since they all did much the same thing. There was little difference in the medicines used by the rural cunning man and the London 'orthodox', licensed physicians. Herbs still made up most remedies. Animal and human products could be found in the official medical *Pharmacopeia* reference books, and all held the same view of the human body as consisting of four fluid humours which, if out of balance, caused illness. The question then was only one of degree. If we remove this artificial boundary between 'folkloric' and 'regular' medicine, it becomes easier to view Wales not as a rural backwater, but as an active participant in the vibrant, international medical culture of the 17th century.

So let's return once more to Meddygon Myddfai: how famous were they *at the time*? Of course they are an important element of Welsh history, and I don't wish to be an iconoclast. But, the first published edition of their texts and accompanying legend didn't actually appear until the early 19th century. Although popular tales and legends about their existence certainly spread in Tudor and Stuart Wales, we don't know how far, how continuously or for how long. So could one dynasty of physicians in a small part of rural Carmarthenshire really have figured much in the day-to-day medical experience of most Welsh people? Do they – *should* they – represent or encapsulate Welsh medicine? I remain to be convinced.

10

WE'RE THE PAROCHIAL WELSH: WHY SHOULD WE TRAVEL?

Katharine Olson

There is an idea that pre-modern Welsh men and women rarely left Wales at all. They were too parochial. Instead, they remained in the villages and valleys of their parents and grandparents. After all, why travel? Their homes, families, and livelihoods were all here. Their worlds were local. They had limited horizons – and, perhaps, could not be bothered. Unless you were a crusader or a king, travel was a great unknown.

In fact, the horizons of Welsh men and women living in the Middle Ages and early modern period were much wider, even international in their scope. Many travelled frequently within England and Wales, far from their own valleys,

churches, and hamlets. They went to visit extended family, neighbours, friends, or acquaintances. They travelled on business, and fairs and markets could also bring people from near and far, turning a tidy profit in Welsh towns and villages. These were places to buy goods, animals, and food, get the latest gossip, hear important public announcements, and see the local sights. People travelled too on pilgrimages throughout England and Wales – from Holywell to Penrhys, St Davids to Llandderfel, and to English destinations like Canterbury and Walsingham.

But centuries before 1800, the Welsh had also followed the call of the sea much further afield. From early medieval ships criss-crossing the Irish Sea, they also traversed Europe, the Mediterranean, the Middle East, and some were early settlers in the New World. Through trade and settlement, they came to know the outside world, and showed an interest and awareness in it. Whether as pilgrims, sailors, crusaders, tradesmen, men of fortune, clerics, or settlers, many Welsh people ventured far beyond Wales. Even those who had not done so heard stories of far-off places, or knew people who had travelled further afield. Such tales were just the thing for long winter evenings, or (if particularly colourful) the local gossips: armchair tourism at its best.

THE DANGERS OF THE JOURNEY

Next time that you're waiting in line at the airport for an international flight, spare a thought for the medieval or early modern Welsh traveller. Frequent flyers today have it remarkably easy in comparison. Travellers to far-flung destinations in Europe and the Middle East had a far more dangerous (and much longer) trip than we could ever imagine today.

Even close to home, humdrum trips such as a journey to the fair were potentially hazardous. The Denbigh fair, for example, brought people from across North Wales and the Marches. But it was not easy to get to: the poet Iolo Goch warned of the dangers of the narrow road, thornbushes, and hedgerows. Other possible perils included theft or random violence. Accidents also happened, due to excessive drinking or the hazards of the road. In 1609, Thomas Hughes left the Abergele fair, but never made it home, drowning in a river near Rhuddlan on the way.

But people from Wales who travelled abroad faced many more potential perils and obstacles. Plenty of these we take for granted today, from fast, safe transport to reasonable food and clean water on demand. There was no guarantee of any of these for our travellers.

Travel could take weeks, even months, depending on the route. If you did not have the money for a horse, you often had to walk. Most roads were not paved – they could be muddy, dusty, or icy depending on the season, not to mention full of stones and brambles. Travellers drowned crossing rivers en route. Certain trips could be taken partly by ship, but these were far from reliable either – wooden and rickety, they could (and did) sink in fierce storms. Even getting as far as Calais could be difficult: the ship of one medieval Welsh traveller was cast on to land no less than three times in rough weather.

Health and hygiene also were problems. People died from food poisoning, starvation, sickness, infected sores, and more: finding food, clean water, and medical care were major problems. Nor did a warm, dry place to sleep present itself every evening; travellers often slept outside in the cold, risking exposure and hypothermia.

Travellers were at the mercy not only of the weather but other people too. Robbers and brigands preyed on groups of travellers. Women worried about rape or other violence. Travelling through a country wracked by war meant running the risk of getting hurt, killed, or thrown into jail as a spy. People worried about these dangers whilst away, and their dependants worried about them in turn. For example, when Sir Edward Carne went on pilgrimage to Rome, his poet Lewys Morgannwg (at home) fretted about his staying safe from the plague, towns, wars, food poisoning, bullets, quarrels, the spears of robbers, fires, French traitors, and more.

BUSINESS AND ADVENTURE

Yet Welshmen and women still set out on long-distance journeys despite the obvious dangers, for many of the same reasons we go on package tours or business trips today. Men in government, spies, and diplomats needed to cross the Continent on urgent errands for their bosses. Clerics, like Gerald of Wales in the 12th century, travelled on church business, particularly to Rome. Welsh scholars crossed the channel to get to universities in France, Germany, Italy, and elsewhere.

Welsh sailors and traders saw much of the world too. They departed from the Llŷn peninsula, Anglesey, ports in South Wales like Newport, or English ones such as Bristol. Trade with Spain in particular was well established. Spanish leather made in Cordova was highly prized by Welsh nobles, and used for shoes and sword scabbards. Spanish wine also found its way onto Welsh tables. The medieval Welsh poet Dafydd Nanmor talked of how his patron, Rhys ap Maredudd of Tywyn, had fine wine from the vineyards of the southern sea – eighteen shiploads of wine casks in total! Clearly Spanish wine was in demand, as was Spanish pottery – archaeologists have found examples all over Wales, from Gwynedd to Aberystwyth to Pembroke to Abergavenny.

The excellently preserved remains of a medieval ship found in 2002 in Newport also speaks to Welsh trade connections. Dating from the 1460s, the merchant ship's remains tell a story of trade between Wales and various European ports and countries, particularly Portugal. From pottery to cannon balls to shoes to Portuguese and German coins, the discoveries from the remains to date reveal a fascinating and

Of all pilgrimages, they [the Welsh] prefer going to Rome, and when they reach St. Peter's they pray there most devoutly.

Gerald of Wales

international world of trade decades before the famed 1492 voyage of Christopher Columbus.

Fighting in Europe was also nothing new for Welsh soldiers. Welsh spearmen and archers were in demand from at least the 1200s. When Edward I commanded 5,300 Welsh soldiers to go to Flanders in 1297, one Ghent man who visited their camp recorded their weapons and their particular habits – which included drinking a lot, and running around barelegged even in the middle of winter. Soldiers from Wales also fought during the Hundred Years War between England and France (1337–1453) and many were stationed in France up to the mid-16th century. Some won fame, such as Sir Hywel ap Gruffydd (d. c1381), known as 'Sir Hywel of the Axe': so greatly was he respected that Edward the Black Prince was said to provide food every day at his table especially for his legendary axe! Welsh archers also fought at the famed Battle of Agincourt (1415).

> There you saw the peculiar habits of the Welsh. In the very depth of winter they were running about bare-legged… Their weapons were bows, arrows, and swords. They also had javelins. They wore linen clothing. They were great drinkers. They endamaged the Flemings very much. Their pay was too small and so it came about that they took what did not belong to them.
>
> Lodewyk van Velthem
> of Ghent

WELSH PILGRIMS AND CRUSADERS

Others made long and difficult journeys for very different reasons. Welshmen and women went on pilgrimages to visit shrines and relics across Europe and beyond. The three most important destinations to medieval Christians were Santiago de Compostela, Rome, and the Holy Land, the 'three blessed fountains of mercy'. When pilgrims arrived, they prayed for cures from disease, injury, or other maladies, and for forgiveness from their sins. Pilgrims were easy to spot: they wore a special broad-brimmed hat often displaying metal badges, carried a scrip (a pouch for food and valuables), and a staff, or stout stick with a metal toe.

By 1300, if not before, there was an added incentive to go on pilgrimage: earning indulgences. After death, most medieval Christians expected to face some additional punishment for their lifetime sins. Some spent eternity in Hell's torments, but many could expect shorter-term suffering in Purgatory, where your soul was purged and purified of any remaining sins before you could finally enter Heaven.

This is where indulgences came in. While they did not *in themselves* offer forgiveness for sins, they had definite advantages. They offered a reduction of the amount of time you spent suffering in Purgatory in punishment for sins already committed, whether by one day or 10,000 years. They were earned in various ways: going on pilgrimage to certain shrines, aiding in public works, giving towards fundraising campaigns for particular causes, attending masses, saying specific prayers, or doing other good works. If you played your cards well, by the later Middle Ages, you could earn thousands of years' worth of indulgences on pilgrimage.

The closest equivalent of a modern package tour was medieval travel to Santiago de Compostela in Spain. The shrine of St James there was a popular destination for the Welsh, who often went via the route known as *Hynt St Ialm* or *Ffordd Seint Jac:* sailing to Calais, and then walking south through France to Spain. Others sailed to Bordeaux, and walked from there. Many took their lives in their hands, and did almost the whole journey by sea: sailing from Bristol, Plymouth, or London to the Bay of Biscay, then walking to Santiago. From the most popular port, Coruña, it was only forty miles. By the later Middle Ages, this direct route was the most popular: with good winds, you could be there and back again very quickly. In fact, enterprising men could make quite a profit from the pilgrim trade. Special pilgrim ships with quick returns from Coruña, allowing just enough time to visit Santiago, were all the rage. The *Mary of Pembroke* was one of many ships to carry Welsh pilgrims to Santiago in the 1400s.

Rome was another popular destination for Welsh pilgrims. Gerald of Wales wrote that it was the favourite pilgrimage of the Welsh. Rome was particularly popular from 1300, when the Pope issued indulgences for those who came to the first Jubilee that year. Eventually jubilees were held every 25 years. Sir Harry Stradling of St Donat's went on a pilgrimage to Rome during the 1475 Jubilee. He wrote to his wife in Wales describing the hard journey, and his delight in receiving an indulgence; it made him 'as clean as the day that I was born.' Unfortunately he died before returning home.

Welsh people got to Rome by various routes. Some travelled from Dover to France, and then headed through the Alps to Italy, or by way of France to another sea port, and sailed the rest of the way there. They often travelled in groups, both for safety and comfort's sake – Huw Cae Llwyd, who went to Rome in 1475, took his teenage son Ieuan along.

The English Hospice in Rome was a popular place to stay, and pilgrims from all over Wales – including Crickhowell, Wrexham, Holyhead, and Carmarthen – lodged together there. They came from all walks of life, too, from sailors to scholars, merchants, gentry, clergy, and the poor. There was, in fact, an established Welsh expatriate community in Rome.

The Holy Land, however, was the ultimate destination for Welsh crusaders

One who would count the relics of Rome
He might as well count all the sea, and the stones...
By one of these I would be absolved [of sin].

Huw Cae Llwyd, c1475

and pilgrims. It was where Christ had lived and died, therefore of great importance for medieval Christians. Welshmen took part in the Crusades, particularly in the 13th century, when many sermons were preached in Wales to recruit crusaders. Getting to the Holy Land from Wales was not easy, though: many drowned crossing the Mediterranean.

Pilgrims who went to the Holy Land were known as palmers, because of the palm branches they brought back with them. Some who went to the Holy Land were even invited to join the exclusive Order of Knights of the Holy Sepulchre. The Stradlings of St Donat's and Siôn ap Morgan of Tredegar, known as 'The Fat Knight', were members. But with the fall of Acre in 1291, it became much more difficult and costly to go to the Holy Land, and pilgrimage to the Holy Land became less popular, but Welsh men and women still went.

THE NEW WORLD

Many Welsh people travelled long distances, only to return home again. Others decided to stay and settle abroad, whether in Rome, France, or elsewhere. Welsh expatriate communities are hardly a modern invention: they have been around for centuries.

But beyond trips to Europe, the Mediterranean, and the Middle East, the prospect of the New World appealed. In fact, the Welsh were very interested in visiting and settling in America long before 1800.

The remains of a medieval ship discovered in 2002 on the banks of the river Usk on Newport

According to legend, Prince Madog was one of them. Supposedly the son of Owain Gwynedd, Prince of Wales (d.1170), he is said to have discovered America centuries before Columbus. According to the tale, he turned his back on the warfare that erupted after Owain's death, and sailed west, eventually discovering a new land. He returned once to his homeland, asking others to join him. Some apparently did, sailing back to the new land, never to be heard of again.

After Columbus's voyage to America, Madog's story gave rise to some even taller tales. In the 16th century, Dr David Powell, the vicar of Rhiwabon, claimed that the place Madog had settled was not America, but Mexico, basing his claims on Welsh words that had supposedly been found in the Aztec language. Fearing Spanish belligerence at home and in the New World, Madog's first supposed 'discovery' of North America was even cited by the English Crown.

Despite the lack of proof that Madog ever made it to America, interest in his story continued. Native Americans in the late 1600s in South Carolina were

The Patagonian wilderness most often associated with Welsh forays abroad

said (incorrectly) to be able to speak Welsh, and at the end of the 18th century, John Evans, a preacher from Caernarfonshire, journeyed through the American wilderness, following the Missouri River in a vain search for the Welsh Native Americans.

Madog's journey faded into legend, but after the voyages of Columbus opened up the New World, many Welsh were among the first pioneers to settle in America. Indeed, just ten years after the first permanent English settlement in America, Jamestown, was founded, and a full three years before the Pilgrims landed in Plymouth, Massachusetts, a little-known Welsh colony in America was established in Newfoundland – over two centuries before the Welsh sailed to Patagonia!

Cambriol, or 'New Cambriol' as it was also known, was the brainchild of Sir William Vaughan (1575-1641) of Golden Grove in Carmarthenshire, who purchased land for it in 1616, and started settling people there the following year. An opportunist, he saw it both as a money-making venture, and an opportunity

to better the lives of poor labourers in South Wales. Newfoundland, he decided, would be an easier and less costly venture than Virginia, and planned a plantation of his own. A variety of townships, all with Welsh names, sprang up: Cardiff, Pembroke, Cardigan, and Brecon. But Cambriol's days were numbered: after some 20 years or less, its inhabitants had had enough. The climate was too forbidding, the soil too infertile, they were vulnerable to attacks from the French and others, and they eked out only a bare living from the fishing trade. They abandoned the settlement and returned to Wales.

However, others followed their lead, especially Welsh Baptists and Quakers. Led by John Miles, the founder of the first Baptist church in Wales (at Ilston, in Gower), a group of Baptists settled in Massachusetts in the 1660s. The group settled in a township south of Boston, calling it 'Swanzey'. Today you can still visit Swansea, as well as Pembroke in Massachusetts. Other Welsh Baptists, mainly from Radnorshire, settled in modern Delaware in 1701 on 30,000 acres of land that they named 'The Welsh Tract', some moving on to South Carolina in the mid-1730s. Welsh Quakers, many from Meirionnydd, also settled in America. Many followed William Penn to Pennsylvania in 1682. Their legacy is obvious today: from Bryn Mawr (also a college), to Denbigh, Radnor, Bala, Cynwyd, Narberth, Tredyffrin, and Berwyn, Welsh place names remain common, particularly near Philadelphia. Indeed, so many Welsh people lived in the Philadelphia area that from 1721 Welsh-language books were printed there.

Welsh settlement did not end in Philadelphia. From Canada to Utica (New York), Virginia, Ohio, Kansas, Minnesota, and Iowa, other settlements flourished. In the 1800s more and more Welsh people emigrated to North America. But by that time, their desire to see a new world was hardly new. They were simply following in the footsteps of centuries of Welsh travellers before them.

TIMELINE

1096: the first Crusade begins

1170: supposed voyage of Prince Madog

1300: first Jubilee in Rome

1492: voyage of Christopher Columbus

1607: Jamestown settlement founded in Virginia

1617: Cambriol settlement begins in Newfoundland

1660s: Welsh baptists settle in Massachusetts

1682: William Penn and other Quakers settle in Pennsylvania

11

MONMOUTH – WALES OR ENGLAND?

Chris Williams

Because I was born in Monmouthshire, the nationality of the county and its people has always been a subject close to my heart. When I was a child, I had little doubt that I was Welsh. It was a source of puzzlement to me, therefore, that many atlases appeared to place Monmouthshire in England, by marking the England / Wales border to the west of the county, on the boundary with Glamorgan.

When English friends suggested that Monmouthshire was really in England, I was indignant. My favoured rugby team, Newport RFC, might be affiliated to both England's RFU and the Welsh Rugby Union, but (with the exception of England international prop forward Colin Smart, whose place in rugby foklore was assured when he celebrated victory over France with a swig of aftershave!) the ambition of its players was surely to pull on the red jersey with its Prince of Wales feathers!

In my professional life as a historian I became embroiled in the issue. When Queen Victoria died in 1901 public spirited individuals had set up the 'Victoria County History of England' to produce authoritative historical surveys of the English shires. Monmouthshire was on their list, so when a group of Welsh enthusiasts started a similar project for the counties of Wales in 1902 they left Monmouthshire alone.

Monmouthshire Wales, not England: Blaenavon-born Ken Jones, Newport RFC's legendary Welsh international winger 'the theory that Monmouthshire is an English county, first conceived by error, received without examination, and settled at last by an indolent consent, has ... no historical or legal foundation, and must be pronounced a geographical blunder'

Thomas Nicholas: *Annals and Antiquities of the Counties and County Families in Wales (1872)*

Neither English nor Welsh venture bore fruit, so nearly a century later I was one of a number of people who began planning and plotting the *Gwent County History*, four volumes of which have been published, taking the story from 'the beginnings' to 1914.

Investigating the history of my native county has involved confronting the question that baffled me as a child: why, if most of the people of Monmouthshire thought themselves Welsh (as I am sure they did by the 1960s and 1970s when I was growing up), did geographers persist for so long in depicting the county as part of England?

A MATTER OF LEGALITY

The answer takes us back to the so-called 'Acts of Union' of 1536 and 1543 which brought Wales and England together. 'So-called' because it was only after the Scots and the Irish had had their own 'Acts of Union' (in 1707 and 1800 respectively) that historians decided to elevate Wales's status by rebadging the original legislation.

The point was that both the Scots and the Irish had had parliaments which had passed legislation to unite with England. In Wales nothing similar had occurred. Wales had been conquered by the end of the 13th century and thereafter administered as both the 'Principality' (most parts of the north and west of the country) and the 'March' (mostly the southern and eastern parts, spilling over into what are now the border counties of England).

The Tudor state had decided, for its own stability, to rationalise the governance of both Principality and March by extending the English system of justice, administration and parliamentary representation, based around the county unit, or shire, to all of what we today regard as Wales. New counties were created, and in effect Wales was absorbed into the English state. Certain anomalies remained, but to most intents and purposes there was no longer any need for a recognized line of demarcation or border between England and Wales.

Monmouthshire was one of the new counties. Seemingly for the sake of neatness rather than with any more Machiavellian motive, it was attached to the Oxford circuit for the purpose of the administration of justice. This act, at the time relatively innocuous, was the source of all the later confusion. As Monmouthshire was linked to counties of western England, so it became possible to regard it as English.

I knew this even as a child, and was fond (as most Welsh patriots, such as Thomas Nicholas, were) of pointing out that the Tudors had not intended to transform Monmouthshire's nationality. I now know that this was an anachronistic argument: Wales had ceased to exist as a separate political unit – in many ways *all* of Wales had become part of England – and in so far as expert legal opinion on the matter was sought, it always pronounced that Monmouthshire was part of England.

In fact, research by one of the scholars working on the next volume of the *Gwent County History* has shown that Monmouthshire's status remained legally English until the reorganization of local government in the 1970s.

The Tudors had had no idea of the later problems they would create with the 'Acts of Union'. But it took until the mid-19th century, when the character of Wales and the Welsh people began to be treated as a political issue, for the issue to surface.

Although Monmouthshire no longer forms a part of the Principality, that portion which is comprised within the great mineral basin is so thoroughly Welsh as regards the character, habits, and language of the larger part of its inhabitants, that it could scarcely have been excluded from this inquiry without injury to the comprehensiveness of the Reports.

Jellinger C. Symons *Reports of the Commissioners of Inquiry into the State of Education in Wales (1847)*

THE CHARACTER OF THE COUNTY

It was those pantomime villains of Welsh history, the education commissioners responsible for the 'Treason of the Blue Books' in 1847, who were amongst the first to draw attention to the anomalous position of Monmouthshire.

In coming to assess the state of education in Wales (and pronounce on the deleterious effects of Nonconformism and the Welsh language) the commissioners decided that they had to include at least the western, industrializing parishes of the county for their report to be coherent. These covered less than a third of the land area of the county, but included about two-thirds of its population.

Those who disagreed with the commissioners' conclusions nevertheless shared their view of the essential Welshness of many Monmouthshire people. Sir Thomas Phillips (of Newport Rising fame) thought the county Welsh 'on account of the origin, language and character of the native inhabitants' and there was no denying that Welsh continued to be spoken by many residents of Monmouthshire.

The problem was that if language was to remain the key criterion by which nationality was judged, then by the late 19th century Monmouthshire was becoming more and more English, as the linguistic frontier shifted steadily westward.

The very faces of the people are evidence of their Taffyhood... their voices and names are redolent of *leeks*.

Blackwood's Edinburgh Magazine (1854) on Monmouthshire

Confusion abounded as a result. The Reverend James Francis regretted, in 1839, that the Newport Rising had taken place in 'the Principality of which he was a native', but two years later publicly admitted 'he knew not whether to class Newport as belonging to England or Wales'.

On its foundation in 1892, the *South Wales Argus*, seemingly in contradiction of its own title, conceded that Monmouthshire was in England. On August 5, 1914, it proclaimed 'England Declares War Against Germany'. The men of the county might be told that 'Your Country Needs You' but it was not clear precisely which country that was!

Part of the problem was that the British state appeared inconsistent in its treatment of the county. Often regarded as the first piece of modern legislation to treat Wales as a distinct unit, the Sunday Closing (Wales) Act of 1881 did not apply to Monmouthshire. The attempt to include the county was thwarted when the Attorney-General gave his view that it was in England.

The legislation itself produced anomalies, when would-be drinkers living on the Glamorgan side of the river Rhymney simply had to cross a bridge to find alcoholic refreshment, but Monmouthshire was not brought under the act for a further 40 years.

Yet Monmouthshire was included in the Welsh Intermediate Education Act of 1889, and when the disestablishment of the Anglican Church reached the statute books in 1914, the county was subject to this as well.

THE DESTINY OF GWENT

It might seem that by the First World War the tide was moving in one direction. Monmouthshire County Council (established 1888) might have both the Welsh dragon and the English lion on its coat of arms but it generally backed the 'Welsh' identity of the county.

St David's Day was celebrated in Monmouthshire with a half-day holiday from 1914, and what is now Chepstow racecourse was offered as a potential and much more sensible site than the one eventually chosen for the National Library of Wales.

The county council also supported the University of Wales (although the closest college would be the ambiguously titled University College of South Wales and Monmouthshire – considerably more elegant than today's bland 'Cardiff University').

Monmouthshire's MPs belonged to the Welsh Parliamentary Party, and Monmouthshire men such as William Brace, Thomas Richards and Vernon Hartshorn played key roles in the leadership of the South Wales Miners'

Federation. The coal seams of the South Wales coalfield, after all, took no notice of county or national boundaries.

So even though various Attorneys-General and other prominent legal eagles might continue to hold that Monmouthshire, legally, was English, the Welsh patriots were winning the battle for the county's destiny.

REDEFINING WALES

Such belief that Monmouthshire was really Welsh stemmed not only from prizing its remaining pockets of Welsh speaking, or studying its ancient place-names. In the fast moving world of 'American' Wales, as the Welsh language retreated westward and as tens of thousands of migrants (mostly English) came to settle in the county, this did not offer enough support.

Instead, the very definition of what it meant to be Welsh was being reconfigured, around politics, religion and popular leisure.

In politics, Monmouthshire, like the rest of Wales, shifted left, first towards liberalism and later socialism. Aneurin Bevan (born Tredegar, 1897) is perhaps the county's most famous product, and no one would have dared suggest he was English!

In religion, Monmouthshire greeted the Evan Roberts religious revival of 1904–05 with as much fervour as more obviously Welsh-speaking areas further west.

And some forms of popular leisure deliberately connected the county to its Welsh heritage, such as holding the National Eisteddfod in Newport (1897) and Abergavenny (1913). To the *South Wales Argus* in 1897, the arrival of the 'Stedvurd' (as the newsboys pronounced it) was 'an act of repatriation', revealing that 'ties of race ... cannot be over-ridden by the fiat of monarch or the vote of Parliament'.

More regular forms of patriotic endorsement were to be found on a different kind of *maes* ('field'). Rugby offered all, irrespective of origins or language, a rewarding allegiance, for it was claimed in 1892 that 'nowhere is football more popular than Monmouthshire... the county is the home of the Rugby game'.

So Lloyd George might fume at the 'Newport Englishmen' who stood in his way in 1896 when he tried to transform the Welsh Liberal Party with the *Cymru Fydd* ('Young Wales') programme which backed Home Rule, but Rodney Parade, Newport was the venue for the only home rugby international in the 1894 championship, when 15,000 supporters of 'morbid footballism' (another Lloyd George slur) witnessed Wales beat Scotland.

Monmouthshire's legal status as technically English, then, was not

Tredegar-born Aneurin Bevan
ventures underground

something that prevented the people of the county (well, most of them) from being seen and seeing themselves as more clearly Welsh. As the poet Islwyn had written, *'bob amser nid rhaniadau anian yw rhaniadau daearyddiaeth'* ('the divisions of temperament are not always those of geography.')

ISLWYN

Gwyllt Walia ydywt tithau, Mynwy gu!	*(Wild Gwalia art thou also, dear Monmouthshire!*
Dy enw'n unig a newidiaist ti	*It is only thy name which thou hast changed.*
Ein heiddo ydywt trwy hynafol rodd	*Thou art ours by ancient gift,*
Ac ysbryd Gwlad y Rheieidr ni chyffrodd	*And the spirit of the Land of the Waterfalls never stirred*
Ar dy fynyddoedd, ni'th adawodd di	*In thy mountains, never left thee*
Pan fynnai Lloegr dy restru ymysg ei siroedd hi.	*When England insisted upon listing thee among her shires.)*

From 'Cymru', in *Gwaith Barddonol Islwyn* (Wrexham, 1897), p. 381.

Not all Welsh patriots (particularly not those for whom cultural and linguistic purism remained the gold standard of Welshness) could comfortably accept the kind of Welshness developed in Monmouthshire (and, increasingly, in the valleys and ports of Glamorgan). However, there was no serious prospect of home rulers or later advocates of devolution leaving Monmouthshire out of the equation. By 1911, the county contained one-sixth of Wales's total population, and was home to much of its industrial base.

So when, finally, in the 1970s, serious questions began to be asked of the system of government, the answers confirmed the county as legally Welsh. Monmouthshire was replaced by the more obviously Welsh title of Gwent (with minor boundary changes), and the voters of the new county were invited to deliver their verdict on the Government of Wales Bill at the March 1, 1979 referendum. They were unenthusiastic, but then so was the rest of Wales.

In 1997 enthusiasm was slightly greater, and the National Assembly for Wales became a reality in 1999. It now has jurisdiction over, not Gwent, but the unitary authorities that cover the former county: Blaenau Gwent, Caerphilly, Newport, Torfaen and (just to sustain the possibility for future confusion) Monmouthshire.

So, geographers now know where to draw the boundary between England and Wales, the regional rugby side for Newport (Gwent) affirms its Welshness by being labelled the 'Dragons', and the National Eisteddfod visits on a more regular basis. But in the light of my childhood worries, I'm taking no chances with the future: my three sons have all been born in Glamorgan, just in case this process ever goes into reverse gear!

A boundary is essentially a matter of consciousness and experience, rather than of fact and law.

Anthony Cohen,
sociologist (1998)

Monmouthshire Wales, not England: Newport-born Jason Tovey of the Newport-Gwent Dragons

KEY DATES IN THE HISTORY OF MONMOUTHSHIRE

1536 and 1543: The 'Acts of Union' extend English legal and administrative systems to both the Principality and the March of Wales. The new county of Monmouthshire is attached to the Oxford Circuit.

1881: the Welsh Sunday Closing Act is not applied in Monmouthshire

1889: the Welsh Intermediate Education Act is applied in Monmouthshire

1920: Church of England disestablished in Monmouthshire (following act of 1914)

1921: Sunday Closing is extended to Monmouthshire

1974: Monmouthshire is replaced by Gwent

1979: The people of Gwent vote with those of the rest of Wales on the government's devolution proposals

1996: Gwent is abolished and replaced by unitary authorities, one of which is named Monmouthshire

1999: All of what was once Monmouthshire / Gwent comes under the control of the National Assembly for Wales

12

WAS INDUSTRIAL WALES ONLY SOUTH WALES?

Kathryn Ellis

Wimbledon, Marconi and Christopher Columbus. What do they have in common ? Each hides the credit that should go to North Wales. Lawn tennis was invented near Rhuthun; David Hughes of Corwen transmitted radio waves 17 years before Marconi's wireless telegraph, and every schoolchild knows that Prince Madog discovered America! But even within Wales itself, the innovations of the north are in danger of being forgotten. When 'the valleys' can be used as shorthand for the whole nation, it is easy to think that our industrial past belongs only to the south.

Easy, too, to see why. By the middle of the 19th century, South Wales was an industrial powerhouse. Merthyr Tydfil, the Rhondda and Cardiff were names familiar throughout the world. But a different part of Wales had also gone through the industrial experience, and although places in the north-east such as Rhiwabon, Bersham and the Greenfield Valley might not be quite so familiar in the tale of the country's past, they too deserve credit as cradles of modern Wales.

QUAKERS, IRON AND WAR

Industrialisation came early to the north-east, and one example is the exploitation of iron. The Industrial Revolution was everywhere a gradual development rather than an overnight transformation, but activity undoubtedly accelerated from 1709 when Abraham Darby at Coalbrookdale developed a new technique of using coke for smelting iron. This was to revolutionise the industry by freeing it from the dependence on charcoal. But it was some decades before the technique was widely known and established. At first Darby jealously guarded the innovation, only informing certain associates, often those who shared his Quaker beliefs. Fortunately for North Wales, one of these Quakers was Charles Lloyd of Dolobran. He was working a site at Bersham, near Wrexham, and by December 3, 1721 the diary of his clerk, John Kelsall, shows that the new technology had reached this part of Wales:

> Bersham Furnace ceased this day blowing with charcoal and went on blowing with coakes for potting.

Only traces of its industrial past remain at Bersham now, but it was once the site of a world-renowned iron business and probably the first individual ironworks to come to prominence in Wales. The height of its success came during the late 18th century under the stewardship of the Wilkinson family: firstly Isaac who moved to Bersham from Lancashire in 1753 and then his more famous son John a decade later.

The entrepreneurial talents of the Wilkinsons drove Bersham's success, but they were favoured by economic circumstances too. The ironworks specialised in two main products.

Firstly, armaments in huge quantities, which were much in demand during a period that included the Seven Years' War, the American War of Independence and the Napoleonic Wars. John Wilkinson had developed and then patented machinery to bore cannon and he made the most of this by selling to whichever side would buy. Secondly, by the 1770s he was able to turn the technique of his cannon-boring machine to further advantage. It was only Wilkinson who could produce cylinders 'with the truth and exactness' required for the new steam engines of Boulton and Watt. For the next 20 years, Bersham produced virtually all the cylinders that Boulton and Watt required, and the ironworks prospered. Unfortunately the bubble eventually burst and a combination of family feuding, greed, fraudulent dealings and developing competition brought the Bersham monopoly to an end. Bersham's heyday was over, and the works were closed by the end of the 18th century, but for a brief period, in the words of Aiken's *A Description of the Country from Thirty to Forty Miles round Manchester* (1795) Wilkinson's '...very ingenious mechanism brought it to succeed in a wonderful manner, so that the works may be reckoned among the first of the kind in the kingdom'.

TRANSPORT AND COMMUNICATION

Sustained industrial success is dependent on good communication routes: raw materials and finished products need to reach their markets at a competitive price. This proved to be one of the greatest challenges to industrial advance in north-east Wales. In this pre-railway age there was heavy reliance on inland waterways and the construction of canals became a national obsession.

Deprived of nearby deep-water ports since the silting up of Chester, the time and cost of transportation challenged all industrial entrepreneurs in the north. In South Wales, canals were constructed to link to the ports of Swansea, Neath, Cardiff and Newport. The same was true of the north-east. The Ellesmere Canal Company was formed in 1791 to promote the making of a canal to link the Mersey, Dee and the Severn to a sea outlet at Ellesmere Port, and so to provide:

> ...a safe and easy communication for the Carriage of Goods and merchandise by water from Liverpool to Shrewsbury and to a great extent of intermediate Country not at present accommodated by any other inland Navigation and will be of a great public utility.

After much discussion the route was agreed and an Act of Parliament to begin the project was passed two years later. Thomas Telford was appointed as the 'General Overlooker' and wrote to a friend:

> It is the greatest Works I believe, that is in hand in the kingdom and will not be completed for many years to come.

Pontcysyllte Aqueduct

Telford was in fact being unduly optimistic. Financial and topographical problems meant that the canal never reached Chester or Shrewsbury, and the anticipated economic impact was never made.

But during the course of its construction all kinds of technical problems were overcome in a way which illustrates the spirit and innovation of the time. The most remarkable was the creation of the Pontcysyllte Aqueduct which carried the canal over the River Dee. Aqueducts were an old idea, but this one, the brainchild of Thomas Telford, was designed on 'a principle entirely new' with the canal carried across the River Dee in iron troughs. It took ten years to construct but eventually in 1805 this remarkable structure stood 1007 feet long and 97 feet above the river bank: the longest earthwork in Britain at the time. The Report of the General Assembly at the time declared:

> We do not know of any other Aqueduct of equal magnitude over which a navigable canal has been carried.

Today it continues to dominate the landscape of the area, and its significance has been recognised with World Heritage status.

THE GREENFIELD VALLEY

Iron and coal dominated the area around Wrexham, which was the largest town in Wales for much of the 18th century. But just as in the south, industrial development in the north-east as a whole was remarkably diverse. Metalworks, potteries, cotton mills and lead mines all flourished.

The principal focus of this varied industrial activity was the mile-long Greenfield valley in Flintshire with its centre at Holywell. The icons and the miraculous healing powers associated with St Winifred's Well meant that this had long been a place of Catholic pilgrimage. Now it became a shrine to a new kind of visitor: the industrial entrepreneur.

The main focus here was on cotton and the non-ferrous industries of copper and brass. All kinds of manufactured goods emerged from the valley, from copper sheets to line the bottoms of ships to kettles, milk pans and even the copper rods (manillas) worn by negroes around ankles or arms and which could be sold to traders in the bartering system surrounding slavery. By the middle of the 18th century, Liverpool had become the largest slave-trading port in Britain and the industrialists of the Greenfield Valley were near enough, and willing, to take advantage of the profits to be made from human traffic.

The success of the valley attracted industrialists of international repute. Thomas Williams of Llanidan, the 'Copper King' (1737-1802) who dominated

Parys Mountain

the British copper industry, recognised the profit to be made and set up works at the lower end of the valley to process copper from the mines on Parys mountain in Anglesey during the 1780s. During this period Williams's industry became the largest supplier of copper and brass articles in the world. But once again success was short-lived. By the nineteenth century mines and mineral resources were exhausted, there was little new investment and the focus of the industry moved elsewhere. The story of iron would become Merthyr instead of Bersham; Swansea, and not Holywell, would be 'Copperopolis'.

FACTS AND FIGURES

Pontcysyllte Aqueduct opened in 1805 at a cost of £38,498 10s 11d. The longest earthworks in Britain at 1007ft

Wrexham: Population in late 17th century of 3,225 and was the largest town in Wales

1700–1750 Flintshire had the fastest population growth rate in Britain: 52%

Formal Trade Unionism comes to Wales in 1830 with the formation of the friendly Associated Coalminers' Union at Bagillt, Flintshire

THE PRICE OF SUCCESS

Industrialisation can mean modernisation and progress, but in these early years rapid change brought hardship and disease. People flocked to the furnaces and coalmines, but by the 1820s living and working conditions were generating waves of protest throughout Wales. The familiar names are again in the south – the Merthyr Rising or the Rebecca Riots. But the north-east too had a part to play.

The coalfield of the region was overtaken by protest in the closing months of 1830. A short strike by colliers at Hawarden in December for increased wages was successful, but by Christmas Day, the men were out again. Demands relating to pay and conditions struck a common chord and the Flintshire miners marched through the coalfield into Denbighshire, gathering up support as they went. A near riot took place between yeomanry and the miners at Cinder Hill in Rhosllannerchrugog, but by December 30, under the mediation of Sir Watkin Williams Wynn, the so-called 'Wrexham riots' were over. The owners accepted the strikers' demands relating to wages and some sense of peace was restored.

This was the first large-scale strike in Wales and the intention may even have been to turn it into part of a general strike. This never materialised but the unity of action of the North Wales coalfield heralded an emerging class consciousness across the country. The formation of unions became legally possible after 1825, and were soon a key element in the struggle between workers and employers. During times of depression Flintshire colliers found work in the Lancashire mines and so must have been aware of the Friendly Associated Coalminers Union which was formed there in 1830. They began to organise at home, and by November 1830 a branch of the union existed at Bagillt, in Flintshire. John Davies calls this 'the first evidence of formal trade unionism in Wales', and by April 1831, under the influence of William Twiss, a union organiser from Bolton, union clubs had multiplied and were formally affiliated to the National Association for the Protection of Labour (NAPL). In the parish of Rhiwabon alone, there were said to be 2,500 members.

So here Flintshire led the way and was followed in the south by the establishment of union lodges after the Merthyr Rising in June 1831. Communication between workers in north and south is noted in a report to the Home Office in 1831 which records itinerant preachers of unionism active in the Rhiwabon area – particularly Twiss, and William Hughes of Rhos. The informant notes that Twiss 'went from hence to South Wales carrying with him the whole of the cash collected at the various Depots and arrived there a short time previous to the disturbances at Merthyr Tydfil'.

WORKING CONDITIONS

An editorial of the *Chester Courant* following the Wrexham riots noted that '… the working classes are disposed to complain' and they had much to complain about. It would be a long time before the unions and more enlightened employers eased the horrors of early industrial life: long hours, and conditions that risked the lives and broke the health of workers. Some of these workers, of course, were children. In the north, as in the south, they had to come early to working life. A government *Report on the Employment of Children and Young Persons in Mines and Mineral Works* was produced in 1842. The section on North Wales records the 12-hour days worked by children, often as young as six years of age. The Rhiwabon coal seams were thin, enabling children to start work at a younger age than in the thicker seams of the south. Still H. H. Jones, the author of the North Wales *Report* notes how on coming up to the surface he 'was surprised and pleased to observe the alacrity with which they went to play; they were quite alive to their amusements, and enjoyed themselves with all the vivacity of youth and health, preferring their games to going home to their food.' And when Mr James Jones of the British Iron Company's colliery at Rhiwabon was asked if the boys become wearied at their tasks, his response was: 'No, they bound like young goats from their work to their play'.

THE BALANCE SHIFTS

Before long, of course, the balance of industrial output and of union activity would shift dramatically to the south, and there remain until the early influence of the north-east was largely forgotten. In 1933, Wrexham-born academic Professor A. H. Dodd wrote a seminal work: *The Industrial Revolution in North Wales*. Dodd's rationale for his book on the north was to look at regions which had not been investigated as fully as he felt they should. His view was that there was a need to redress the balance and to show the impact of the 'quickening of economic life' in an area which had 'long been cut off by a geographical and cultural barrier from the mainstream of economic development'. As he went on to show, the area's 'economic backwardness and its difficult physical geography were no deterrents in that age of miracles, for they spelt cheap labour, untapped ores, and rapid mountain torrents'. Dodd set the area on the historical map but later research remains largely hidden in unpublished theses and dissertations. The north-east was eventually dwarfed by the size and scale of the south, and the story of industrial Wales became the story of South Wales. But the seeds of industrial glory were sown as much in Wrexham and Holywell as in Merthyr and the Rhondda. We may never persuade the United States to recognise its debt to Prince Madog, or move the Lawn Tennis Association from its comfortable home in London, but it would be a pity if we in Wales were to forget our industrial roots in the north.

KEY DATES

1709: Abraham Darby at Coalbrookdale begins to smelt iron with coke instead of charcoal

1721: Bersham Iron Works begins to smelt iron with coke

1753: Wilkinson family take over the Bersham works

1805: Opening of Pontcysyllte Aqueduct

1830: Wrexham riots

1831: Merthyr Rising

13

WAS WALES OPPOSED TO THE SLAVE TRADE?

Chris Evans

No one loves a slaver. Our instinctive sympathies lie with the enslaved, not those who oppress them. This is doubly the case in Wales, where we like to think of ourselves as automatically on the side of the downtrodden. That being so, it is easy enough to imagine that the Welsh were enthusiastic about the abolition of the British slave trade in 1807 and the ending of slavery in Britain's Caribbean empire in 1834.

But was that really the case? There are certainly shining examples of Welsh men and women who devoted themselves to the cause of anti-slavery. In 1779, before any organised campaign against the slave trade existed, the Methodist preacher William Williams of Pantycelyn published a Welsh translation of *A narrative of the most remarkable particulars in the life of James Albert Ukawsaw Gronniosaw, an African prince*, one of the first written accounts of the Middle Passage by a survivor. That we know; we know far less about how Gronniosaw's *Narrative* was received by Welsh readers. It is a common problem for historians. In looking at abolitionism our focus falls all too readily on individuals like the poet Edward Williams (Iolo Morganwg) who was passionate in his denunciations of slavery. But who defined the Welsh mainstream at the end of the 18th century? Iolo Morganwg the poet? Or his three now-forgotten brothers, all of whom migrated to Jamaica – and who all became slave owners?

Iolo Morganwg

The best way to assess the strength of Welsh abolitionism is to take its measure against abolitionism in other parts of the British Isles. Focusing on firebrands like Iolo Morganwg tells you more about him than it does about the Welsh population at large. How does Wales as a whole compare?

Not that well. The campaign against the slave trade took off in England in the 1780s with startling speed. It could do so because of the vibrancy of English urban life. England had one of the highest rates of urbanisation in Europe. Lots of people therefore lived in an environment where people and news circulated rapidly. Places like Manchester, which became an instant stronghold of abolitionism, had a cultural infrastructure on which anti-slavery campaigners could build: newspapers, social clubs and philanthropic societies. There was an emergent tradition of civic activism to be harnessed, one that allowed urban-industrial populations to make a political space for themselves, independent of the landlord class that still held sway in rural counties.

The same could not be said of Wales. A veteran abolitionist who toured North Wales in the early 1820s was struck by the political timorousness of the common people; they were 'half a Century behind those of South Wales – and a Century behind those of England'. Things were little better in west Wales. He found the inhabitants of Cardigan mired in 'subordination and ignorance'. Urban backwardness meant a dearth of local anti-slavery societies.

Welsh people did petition against the slave trade, but not in large numbers. In 1792, when Parliament was deluged with abolitionist petitions, just 20 of the 519 that arrived in Westminster originated in Wales. Moreover, Welsh petitions were often conservative in form, emerging from formal county meetings. These were gatherings of the gentry elite and respectable freeholders, not of the 'inhabitants at large' – even women! – who flocked to add their signatures to petitions in English towns. The innovative campaigning style to be found there was less evident in Wales. Only Swansea, which could boast up-to-the-minute urban facilities, could claim a continuous abolitionist presence. But Swansea, which was both a fashionable seaside resort and a burgeoning industrial centre, was very much a place apart. Elsewhere in Wales, anti-slavery stuttered for long periods.

The contrast with Scotland is also telling. In many ways Scotland was not promising territory for the abolitionist cause. There were strong ties to the West Indies, where Scots were proverbially numerous as plantation managers, and Glasgow was one of the Atlantic's principal ports, specialising in the trade in slave-grown tobacco. Yet in other respects Scotland was well equipped to sustain abolitionist agitation. It had a strong urban tradition and universities that were centres of Enlightenment learning. These influences may do something to explain the success of the petitioning movement in 1788 and 1792. The petition from Edinburgh in 1792 had over 10,000 signatures; Manchester was the only provincial centre to muster more. Scottish conditions also nourished local anti-slavery associations well before any appeared in Wales. By 1792 there were abolitionist societies in Glasgow, Edinburgh, Paisley, Perth and Aberdeen. Thirty years would pass before the foundation of the Swansea and Neath Anti-Slavery Society in 1822, the first such body in Wales and the only one of any substance.

By the 1820s, Welsh Nonconformists had started to take a keener interest in the slavery question, but Welsh Dissenting congregations, despite a growing number of adherents, exerted little political power. In the early 19th century the Anglican Church was the political as well as the religious establishment; the chapels enjoyed far less leverage. The situation in Scotland was rather more favourable. The Presbyterian Church was the state church and it was friendlier to anti-slavery than was the Anglican Church in Wales. Several leading members of the Church of Scotland were eminent in the abolitionist campaigns of the 1820s and 1830s. Dr Andrew Thomson, the minister at the prestigious St George's Church in Edinburgh, played a decisive role in converting the British movement from 'gradualism' (the hope that slavery could be abolished at some point in the future when conditions were right) to 'immediatism'(the conviction that slavery was a moral abomination that should be terminated at once, come what may). No one from Wales ever exercised influence of that sort.

That reflected a wider reality, despite the efforts of many resolute Welsh activists. Wales, sad to say, played no significant role in the struggle against slavery.

HOW DO IRELAND AND WALES COMPARE?

Ireland's role in the history of Atlantic slavery is much like that of Wales: mixed. Ireland, or more accurately the province of Munster, was an important part of the wider supply network that kept plantation agriculture functioning. Wales helped to clothe slaves, Ireland kept them fed. Cattle raised in the south-west of Ireland were driven to the slaughterhouses of Cork, where their carcasses were dismembered and their meat salted and barrelled up for export. Special care had to be taken in salting the beef, for much of it was destined for the Caribbean where it would be eaten by slaves. The sugar islands – the French islands in particular, for planters there were legally mandated to include beef in their slaves' weekly ration – were a captive market, literally so, for Irish beef.

Irish anti-slavery was akin to the Welsh: patchy and inconsistent. Ireland could not match the density of anti-slavery organisation to be found in England, but major centres like Dublin and Belfast sustained anti-slavery bodies and a lively abolitionist literature. Irish abolitionists were fortunate in that the commanding political figure of the era, Daniel O'Connell, embraced their cause so wholeheartedly. Indeed, the 'Liberator' fought the general election of 1831 on the slogan 'Reform and Negro emancipation'. Welsh politics had no one to match O'Connell's importance as a national leader, nor his commitment to 'Negro emancipation'.

Irish abolitionism was more potent than its Welsh equivalent but it was also a divisive issue. Daniel O'Connell's sincere commitment to the cause brought him into conflict with many émigré supporters. Emancipation did not sit well with the toxic racism to which Irish-Americans were prone.

DID WALES THEN CONTRIBUTE TO ATLANTIC SLAVERY?

The major slaving ports of the 18th century, Liverpool and Bristol, were close at hand but there is no evidence that any slaving expedition left a Welsh harbour. This is probably because Welsh merchant communities were too small to furnish the capital needed to fit out such a major undertaking. But like most regions that bordered the Atlantic, Wales had a contribution to make to the enslavement and exploitation of African peoples.

Slaves were expensive to acquire; those who wanted to buy captives on the African coast had to make payment in goods that local merchants wanted. Copper was one of them. Copper was highly valued in African cultures, as was its alloy brass. That gave Wales, which by the middle of the 18th century was Europe's leading producer of copper, a major role in the slave trade. Factories in the Swansea-Neath district churned out copper and brass articles that were designed specifically for the African market: manillas that were worn around the wrist or ankle as a form of portable wealth, shallow brass bowls called 'Guinea Kettles', and the slender copper rods that went by the trade name of 'Negroes'.

It was no accident that Bristol merchants featured prominently in the early days of the Swansea copper industry. Bristol was Britain's leading slave port in the first half of the 18th century and her 'Guinea' merchants could see the value of investing in copper. The Coster family took over the Melincryddan works in the Neath valley at the start of the 1730s and by the decade's end had moved on to a new, purpose-built copperworks at White Rock, near Swansea. Family members were at the very same time channelling money into the slave trade. Thomas Coster, the head of the family, was part owner of the *Amoretta*, which made seven voyages in the 1730s carrying African prisoners to South Carolina, British North America's most brutal plantation society.

The effective exploitation of the slaves who were landed in the plantation zones of the New World required that they were fed and clothed. Hungry or poorly clad slaves were sickly slaves, and no master wanted slaves who did not live long enough to redeem the price paid for them. It was the clothing of slaves that became a Welsh speciality. Slave labourers in the sugar islands and in British North America were usually dressed in a coarse woollen uniform. The fabric from which jackets and trousers were cut was called 'Negro Cloth' or – revealingly – 'Welsh Plains'. Thousands of yards of this drab material were woven every year in rural households across mid-Wales. Poverty-stricken families in Montgomeryshire and Merionnydd, ground down by rises in rents, rates and tithes, clutched at the opportunity to boost their income by carding, spinning or weaving wool. None of what they produced was consumed locally;

it was sent to far distant markets in the slave Atlantic. The whole purpose of Welsh woollens, one observer went so far as to state in the 1770s, was 'covering the poor Negroes in the West Indies'.

HOW MANY PEOPLE IN WALES OWNED SLAVES?

We don't know. We have no systematic information on slave-holding in the 17th and 18th centuries; we have only scattered knowledge of individuals or families who owned plantations overseas and became conspicuously wealthy because of it. The Pennant family, which owned five plantations in Jamaica (one of them called Denbigh), are probably the best known. They acquired massive wealth through sugar cultivation, wealth that was reinvested in slate quarrying in North Wales and the medieval fantasy of Penrhyn Castle, near Bangor. How many other Welsh families, less ostentatious than the Pennants, benefited from slave labour isn't known.

We have some indication of the extent of slave-ownership at the moment of abolition. When Parliament outlawed slavery in the British Empire in 1833, it was decided to pay compensation – to the slave owners, not the slaves! As a result, there are official papers that list all those who claimed compensation. Using these papers we are able to say that the heir to the Pennant fortune owned 764 human beings at the hour of emancipation, for whose freedom he was paid £13,870 (equivalent to £11.1 million today).

Penrhyn slate quarry

How many other slave holders had roots or residence in Wales is not easily determined. For every claimant who posted a Welsh address – like Revd Edward Picton of Iscoed, Carmarthenshire, who owned 98 slaves on the Aranjuez plantation on Trinidad – there were others who claimed via a business address and whose Welsh affinities are obscured. Only a long and meticulous process of investigation will reveal the true picture.

TIMELINE

1670: The foundation of the Royal African Company marks the beginning of a systematic slave trade by the English. Early shareholders include Welsh gentry families like the Morgans of Tredegar Park and London-Welsh merchants like the brothers Jeffery Jeffreys, MP for Brecon, and John Jeffreys, MP for Radnorshire.

1720s: Britain becomes the biggest slaving nation in the Atlantic world.

1730s: The Swansea copper industry is booming, helped by investment from Bristol. Copper and brass products are important 'trade goods' for Bristol's slave traders.

1780s: Slate quarrying in North Wales takes off, boosted by the wealth that the Pennant family had gained from their Jamaican plantations.

1787: The foundation of the Committee for Effecting an Abolition of the Slave Trade signals the start of an organised campaign against the 'Guinea Trade'.

1788: The first wave of abolitionist petitions arrives in Parliament. A second, even bigger, follows in 1792.

1790s: The British slave trade is at its height.

1807: The abolition of the British slave trade.

1834: Slavery is abolished in Britain's Caribbean empire although ex-slaves are forced to work for their former masters as 'apprentices' for a transitional period.

1838: After further campaigning by anti-slavery activists, apprenticeship is ended.

14

DID WALES HELP TO BUILD THE EMPIRE?

H. V. Bowen

Wales does not loom large in the many histories that have been written about the British Empire. And, on the other side of the coin, the Empire has never featured much at all in writing on the history of Wales. Indeed, few general studies of Wales have ever devoted much attention to the imperial or international dimensions of the Welsh historical experience. When overseas activity is discussed, it is usually in the context of the migrations that took place to North America, Australia, or Patagonia. Little is ever written about Welsh participation in the hard edges of imperial expansion that characterised the British conquest, control, and exploitation of colonies in the Caribbean, Africa, and Asia; and less still is said about the subsequent flows of wealth back into the domestic economy. As a result, for the most part readers will search Welsh history book indexes in vain for the words 'Empire' or 'British Empire', and this is somewhat ironic in view of the fact that it was a London Welshman, the polymath John Dee, who, in 1577, was the first to use the term 'British Empire'.

INVISIBLE IMPERIALISTS

There are a number of reasons why historians have never given much consideration to any relationship that might have existed between Wales and the creation of the British overseas empire.

First and foremost, it is certainly the case that comparatively few Welsh people went overseas and this meant that they often paled into insignificance alongside the English, Irish, and Scots. In India, for example, the Welsh seldom accounted for more than 1% of the entire British presence, and because they were scattered thinly across the subcontinent they were never able to form groups, institutions, and networks like their Celtic cousins.

Yet more than just small numbers explains the invisibility of the Welsh in the historical record of British imperialism. For, as Russell Davies has recently pointed out, Welsh historians have tended to focus their attention on the industrial working classes that emerged during the 18th and 19th centuries. Consequently, there has been a tendency to overlook the middle ranks of society, and especially those restless opportunists who went out into the wider world to oil the wheels of empire as soldiers, sailors, diplomats, doctors, administrators, merchants, and adventurers. Many of these men did in fact carve out successful careers, and in so doing they made notable and diverse contributions to British imperial enterprise. A roll call of their names would be longer than one might think, and this indicates that although the Welsh were few in numbers across the Empire they were in fact well capable of making their mark. Finally, those inclined to view Wales as colony of England have been reluctant to concede that a colonised Welsh people could ever themselves have become active and enthusiastic participants in British imperial enterprise.

Of course, much the same can be said of Ireland and the Irish, but whereas historians of Ireland have explored fully the complexities of the colonised/

Gwyn Alf Williams, the historian who sketched out an 'Imperial Wales'

coloniser relationship, few Welsh historians have ever taken up the challenge. Instead, a blind eye, or at least a partially blind eye, has been turned to Welsh involvement in the Empire. Because of this, we still do not have a clear sight of how, and to what extent, Wales shaped, and was in turn shaped by, the process of imperial expansion.

This cutting adrift of a significant part of the nation's past was noted by the historian Gwyn Alf Williams who sketched out a late 19th-century 'Imperial Wales', 'the sense and feel and smell of which, no doubt because of the formative experience of Depression, Socialism and Welsh Nationalism, Welsh historiography seems largely to have lost.' Is it possible, then, to reconnect with an even more distant imperial past by making the case that Wales was in fact more fully engaged with the Empire than is currently represented in the literature? And can it be said that the internal development of Wales was influenced by the process of imperial expansion as private wealth accumulated overseas filtered back into local economies and societies?

The evidence suggests that the answer to both of these questions is an emphatic 'yes', and an examination of early Welsh interactions with India serves to underline the extent to which Wales was affected by imperial influences, especially those of an economic type. In particular, as the 'English' East India Company carved out an empire for itself (and Britain) in South Asia between 1750 and 1830, Welshmen proved to be as adept as anyone else at making money from the process. Those who survived to return home brought their new wealth with them, and while the effects of their spending were often localised, they did very often leave an indelible imprint on the Welsh landscape.

PASSAGES TO INDIA

It is well known that some prominent figures in British India were from Wales, or at least had Welsh connections. The judge and great oriental scholar Sir William Jones was from an Anglesey family; Sir George Everest, who gave his name to the mountain, may (or perhaps may not) have been born in Crickhowell; Sir William Nott, an uncompromising commander of British forces during the first Afghan War of 1838 to 1842, was born in Neath and grew up in Carmarthen. Such examples are interesting, but cherry-picking them in a random fashion does not help to establish the full extent or strength of any Welsh links with India. Here, it is necessary to look beyond the prominent and the well known, because by seeking out people of the second or third rank we can obtain a much better sense of any group motivations and actions that were at work in Wales.

During the second half of the 18th century, men from Wales went to India primarily to make money. There was not yet any large-scale British missionary activity in India, and thus a vast majority were motivated by the simple desire to acquire the large financial fortune that would set them up for a comfortable retirement. Most of these men were employed by the East India Company but they also traded 'on the side' and exploited many opportunities to conduct private business. They were often ruthlessly single-minded about this and, such was the way of doing things in British India, there can be little doubt that all but the most high minded of them crossed over the line into corruption and illicit activity.

It is certainly the case that a number of men in Wales were inspired by the success of the 'heaven-born general' Robert Clive. 'Clive of India' established British control over Bengal following the battle of Plassey in 1757, and at the same time lined his pockets with a very large amount of money that came from 'presents' he obtained from local rulers. With a domestic political power base that extended into Wales from his home county of Shropshire, Clive was able to use his influence in London to secure entry into the East India Company for a number of his friends and associates. As a result, well-connected fortune-seekers from Breconshire, Montgomeryshire, and Radnorshire were in a prime position to take advantage of the company's expansion in India after 1760.

A key figure within the development of an enduring cross-border East Indian network was Walter Wilkins. After serving as the first governor of Chittagong province during the early 1770s, Wilkins returned home with a large private fortune to settle at Maesllwch castle, near Glasbury. Others from the area followed him in his profitable passage to India and back. Wilkins's brother, Jeffreys, served the Company in Patna; and John Lloyd from Llanwrtyd became a commander of East India Company ships. David Price, born in Merthyr Cynog, was fortuitously placed as the prize agent of the company's army when it stormed Tipu Sultan's citadel at Seringapatam in 1799. On his retirement to Brecon, Price became a well-respected oriental scholar and translator of Persian manuscripts. Harford Jones, from Presteigne, took up company posts at Basra and Baghdad before, in 1807, he became first British Minister Plenipotentiary to be sent to the court of Persia. These men, and others like them, played the system very effectively indeed. They served the empire and the empire served them.

Similar patterns were replicated elsewhere in Wales, most notably in Pembrokeshire where some families built up long traditions of service in India. Often coming from minor gentry or professional backgrounds, those who entered company service were strongly anglicised, and there is little evidence that they either spoke the Welsh language or were self-consciously Welsh in any way. And yet, at the end of their time abroad, these men nearly always returned to Wales, and unlike many of the successful Scots and Irish who served in India they tended not to use their wealth as a means of climbing the social ladder in England. They formed a small and tightly-knit class of local 'nabobs' who as wealthy nouveau riche were often regarded with considerable suspicion and distrust in late-18th century Wales.

EAST INDIAN FORTUNES

The aim of most of those who returned to Wales from India was to become firmly established in landed society. With this in mind they invested heavily in property and the social trappings that they thought should go hand-in-hand with their new-found wealth. Conspicuous consumption was the name of the game. Because of this, it is now possible to identify a surprisingly large number of houses and landed estates that at one time or another were owned by those who had served in the east. These were dotted across a large swathe of territory that stretched south-westwards from the Boultibrooke estate of Harford Jones which straddled the England-Wales border near Presteigne, right through to Tenby where a number of former East India Company servants purchased houses.

Near Llandeilo, the Aberglasney estate was bought for 10,000 guineas in 1803 by a retired East India Company surgeon, Thomas Phillips, who had family connections in the area. During the late-18th century the Upton estate near Pembroke had been purchased by Captain John Tasker. It was said that Tasker had 'acquired a competent fortune' in India and then 'retired to the place of his birth to enjoy it'. From the Company's maritime service, John Jones returned to his roots in Swansea, where in 1794 he bought the striking St Helen's House on a prime coastal site. Jones invested the profits he had accumulated from private trade he conducted when sailing in Asian waters as an officer and commander on board ships of the company.

And it was not just returning Welshmen who snapped up land and property. For political reasons Robert Clive purchased estates in Monmouthshire and Montgomeryshire during the 1760s, and he was followed into Wales by other English nabobs. Most notable perhaps was the idiosyncratic John Zephaniah Holwell who had been temporary Governor of Bengal at the time of the infamous 'Black Hole of Calcutta' episode of 1756. Holwell, who became a JP in Pembrokeshire, invested heavily in the construction of the eccentric Castle Hall, Milford, during the 1770s. Later, Francis Fowke, the Company's

Aberglasney

Paxton's Tower

controversial Resident at Benares between 1775 and 1786, who had amassed a fortune of over £70,000 from trade in opium and diamonds, began the building of a large house on the site of a medieval castle at Boughrood in Radnorshire. No doubt it was Fowke who encouraged his former assistant, John Benn, also to invest part of his £80,000 fortune in Radnorshire. By 1821 Benn had acquired 59 parcels of land, and this added greatly to the concentration of East Indian wealth in the county.

An especially enduring mark was left on the Welsh landscape by William Paxton who, having made a large fortune in Calcutta, spent £40,000 on the Middleton Hall estate, just outside Llanarthne in Carmarthenshire. Paxton built a new mansion, said to be the finest in Wales, laid out ornamental gardens and woodland, and created ponds that were serviced by an elaborate underground network of water pipes. At the time of his death in 1824, his fortune amounted to almost £300,000 and his 2,650-acre estate was dominated by 'Paxton's Tower', or 'Paxton's Folly' as it was known to the locals. The tower, built in honour of Nelson, remains as a prominent local landmark and the National Botanic Garden of Wales is now located on the site of Paxton's former estate.

In some places other forms of investment were undertaken. The Wilkins brothers and John Lloyd used their East Indian fortunes to build up the economic infrastructure of Brecon and the surrounding area. Some of their funds were channelled into the establishment of the Brecon Bank, and they also invested heavily in transport and industry. The transformative local effect of East Indian wealth manifested itself in a rather different way in Llandovery where the former East India Company surgeon, Thomas Phillips (not to be confused with Thomas Phillips of Llandeilo), chose to invest a part of his very substantial fortune. In 1847, when he was in his 80s, Phillips was the main mover behind the establishment and building of the Collegiate Institute, which today exists as the public school known as Llandovery College. And with almost obsessive zeal Phillips diverted much of the rest of his fortune into Welsh education and learning.

These examples illustrate that when the surface of Welsh society is scratched it is possible to uncover significant traces of economic activity that arose directly from British overseas expansion. It would be quite wrong, of course, to suggest that Wales as a whole was somehow transformed by the creation of the Empire, but different regions were certainly tied into wider processes of change and development caused by the exertion of British power in India. Among other things, this calls into question traditional views of Wales as an isolated and inward-looking country that seldom interacted with the wider world.

A WELSH LEGACY IN INDIA

In today's India there are few visible signs of any Welsh involvement in the first phase of the British conquest. However, Thomas Parry, born near Welshpool in 1768, made his mark in more ways than one. Parry found his way to Madras (present-day Chennai) in 1788 but then left company service to take up private trade. He began as a small merchant but over time branched out into shipping, insurance, and industry, eventually becoming one of the most powerful businessmen in southern India. Parry made a large amount of money, but he never saw Wales again because, like many others, he suffered an early death from cholera. Nonetheless, his legacy lives on in the form of his company, which is now India's second oldest business organisation. In Chennai today, 'Parry's' is a defining feature of the urban landscape, with Parry's Corner serving as a key transport junction and providing a central location for the home for what is now E.I.D. Parry (India) Ltd. Parry's company, now part of the Murugappa Group, has interests in more than 200 enterprises ranging from agro-chemicals through to the ceramic bath ware that is adorned with the distinctive 'Parryware' stamp. Indeed, so ubiquitous is Parryware that to go the bathroom in India is nearly always to be reminded of Wales!

15

THE IRISH ARE EVERYWHERE. WHERE ARE THE WELSH?

Gethin Matthews

There is a common belief that emigration from Wales is not numerically significant, particularly when compared with Scotland, or most particularly, Ireland. The general perception is that overseas emigration was relatively unimportant, particularly when you look at the massive amount of migration that occurred *into* the coalfields of South Wales.

I would argue to the contrary, that although Wales never suffered the same trauma as Ireland, a country that lost so many of her people through an emigration that was driven by desperation, Wales lost enough people to leave a mark on the nation. Emigration was significant numerically; it was localised, meaning that certain parts of Wales experienced a substantial impact from emigration; and also the selective nature of emigration meant it changed the make-up of communities back in Wales.

It wasn't just people that crossed the Atlantic – ideas also flowed back and fore between Wales and America (and indeed other emigration destinations such as Australia). One of Wales's foremost historians, Dr John Davies, has argued that the birth of Welsh Nationalist ideas in the late Victorian era didn't take place in Wales, but in the Welsh communities of Pennsylvania and Ohio. That is, it was only by leaving Wales and looking at it from a distance that Welsh people began to see the unity of the country. Some of these individuals returned to Wales, and their ideas helped to shape the way the Welsh at home looked at themselves.

THE NUMBERS GAME

One fundamental question to consider is how many Welsh emigrated in the 19th century, but straightaway there's a problem – the Welsh are consistently under-represented in many official records because they are very often

The Statue of Liberty – a sight for sore eyes

included as English. To give one clear example: according to the United States immigration records, the number of Welsh immigrants to the United States in the period 1820–1950 was just under 90,000. But if you look at the US census return for 1890, you will see that over 100,000 residents of the USA were born in Wales. So, this shows that the figures in the immigration records are totally unreliable. There is, however, one painstaking way of estimating the numbers that emigrated from Wales, and that is to look at the census returns every ten years, and work out how much of the population has gone missing. This has been done for the period 1861 to 1900, showing the emigration rate for each county in Wales and England, and the statistics reveal a number of interesting patterns.

Looking at the percentage of male residents who emigrated, four of the top six counties are Welsh (Breconshire, Pembrokeshire, Montgomeryshire and Monmouthshire), with Glamorgan also in the top ten, and the rest of the western counties of Wales are also high up in the league table. In all, nine of the thirteen counties of Wales are above the average figure for England and Wales of 3.1% of the male population emigrating.

A similar pattern can be seen for female emigration: here, Breconshire is top of the pile, with 5.4% of the ladies of the county emigrating. Welsh counties fill five of the top nine places and again, nine of the 13 counties are above the average for England and Wales.

The figures are in themselves pretty high, but you get some even more striking statistics if you consider that the majority of the emigrants were aged between 15 and 24. If you just consider this portion of the population, then the proportion of emigrants shoots up, to 28% of young Breconshire men, and 26% of young Breconshire women, and 25% of young Monmouthshire men and 18% of young Monmouthshire women. Furthermore, there were significant variations within each individual county. The high emigration rate from Breconshire, Glamorgan and Monmouthshire hides the fact that there were some areas in these counties where emigration was minor and others where the flow of emigrants was a torrent.

As well as the major differences in the patterns of emigration within Wales, there are also significant changes in the picture if you look decade by decade. Within the forty year period 1861–1900 there are a number of patterns, because emigration was not a constant flow. For south-east Wales, the emigration rate was exceptionally high in the 1860s, and remained high in the 1870s and 1880s, before slowing to a trickle in the 1890s – a decade when the coal industry in South Wales was booming. Conversely, the pattern for emigration from Caernarfonshire shows more of a rollercoaster ride: high in the 1860s; very low in the 1870s, very high in the 1880s, and back down to a trickle in the 1890s. This

Welsh fortune-seekers in Colorado in the 1880s

pattern can largely be explained by the emigration (or not) of slate-quarrymen, responding to the relative fortunes of the slate industry in north-west Wales and in the USA. Certainly a lot of slate-workers went from North Wales to the USA in the late 1860s, just after the end of the American Civil War, when there was a lot of rebuilding work to be done in the country.

The basic message here is that there are so many different factors that impacted upon the decision of whether or not to emigrate. These factors varied across different regions of Wales, and they changed with time. For example, when fast and efficient steam-powered boats were introduced for the trans-Atlantic voyage in the 1850s and 1860s, this meant that the cost of emigrating to America came right down. It also opened up the possibility of temporary emigration – before that almost all the human traffic was one-way, from Britain to America, because few people would want to face *two* Atlantic crossings in the cramped and unhygienic conditions of the emigrants' quarters below decks in a sailing ship. But once it became possible to cross the Atlantic in two weeks, emigration ceased to be an irreversible process, which meant that you could get to return home some day to see your family again.

GLOBAL MOVEMENTS; LOCAL PATTERNS

The *local* nature of emigration is a point that needs always to be borne in mind when considering emigration from Wales. There were times and places in Wales when emigration was part of the local culture: an option that was considered and debated within most families. One implication of this is that emigration had a particular and deep impact on certain communities in Wales. A prime example is Merthyr Tydfil and the heads of the valleys area. In the 19th century, Merthyr men turned up all over the globe. Consider this report from the *Cardiff Times* on April 3, 1863:

> Merthyr – Emigration
> … Merthyr's sons & daughters are in America, South & North, California, Queensland, India, Russia, Australia and the Rocky Mountains – an old innkeeper of Caepantwyll lives tranquilly in Mexico and a Dowlais puddler works in Hungary.

Although this report mentions Merthyr's sons and daughters, the emigration from Merthyr was led by men, usually young men, and often highly skilled workers. This reference here to 'puddlers' is indicative – the puddlers were the most skilled and best paid workers in the iron industry. Now, in this period, Merthyr's ironworks were literally world famous: the products of Merthyr's blast furnaces were exported all over the globe, and if you were a Merthyr ironworker, you could be confident that you could walk into a job in an ironworks anywhere in the world because of your town's reputation.

This meant that there was an emigration culture in Merthyr from the start of the industrial period. Emigration was spearheaded by the most highly skilled workers – the furnace managers and the puddlers, but hanging on their coat-tails there would be all kinds of semi-skilled and unskilled labourers. The way it worked was that the furnace managers would establish a new ironworks in the United States, and these works would attract a high number of labourers from the manager's home patch – the men would know that wages and prospects were likely to be better for them in the USA, so off they went.

But the really interesting thing about this report is that it shows how diverse the emigration fever was in Merthyr in the 1860s. Some of the men went to establish ironworks in places other than North America, as evidenced by the reference to Russia and Hungary. But others went to places that had no iron industry, but other opportunities for adventurous young men – such as the gold-fields of California, Australia and the Rocky Mountains. So it seems that although the appetite for emigration was started by the iron industry, once the Merthyr district acquired a taste for emigration, the men of Merthyr were more likely than men from other, less go-getting, parts of Wales to depart for places where there was any kind of opportunity. Indeed, in this period the phrase 'emigration mania' and 'emigration fever' ('y dwymyn ymfudol' in Welsh) is to be found very often in the Merthyr and Aberdare newspapers.

Because the emigration was localised and *selective* – i.e. it affected some elements of the community more than others – over the years emigration worked to change the nature of Welsh communities. One example of how emigration impacted on a region of Wales can be found in North Monmouthshire in the mid-1800s. Up until that time, the area was strongly Welsh-speaking, but this area, like Merthyr, was among the first in Britain to become industrialised, with ironworks running in an arc from Blaenavon to Tredegar. It seems that in the space of a couple of decades, Welsh-speakers became a minority because such a high proportion of the skilled workers emigrated – i.e. in this case it was *emigration* just as much as *immigration* that caused the decline of the Welsh language.

Another industry that saw sizeable emigration from Wales was the tinplate industry. In the 1880s, South Wales was the world-leader in production of tinplate, with three-quarters of its output being exported to America. However in 1890 the USA imposed the McKinley tariff, which slapped a 48% tax on imported tinplate. Overnight, this caused a crisis in the Welsh tinplate industry, and a massive opportunity for the USA's industrial entrepreneurs, who set up new tinplate works, and recruited Welsh workers *en masse*. This inevitably had a substantial impact upon those places that supplied the emigrants. There is one telling example from Swansea: Pentre Estyll chapel was sited literally across the road from the Cwmfelin tinplate works, where most of the chapel's male members worked. Between 1895 and 1898 the chapel lost 229 of its 500 members – almost all to the United States.

Considering the facts and figures that are available, it is clear that emigration from Wales was substantial enough to have a significant impact on Welsh culture, the Welsh economy, and on the life of communities throughout the country.

WHAT ABOUT THE WOMEN?

If the story of Welsh emigration in general is under-researched, then the story of Welsh women emigrants is doubly so. The evidence is dominated by details of what the men did – for example, it was almost always the men who wrote the letters home which were published in Welsh newspapers. So although the figures indicate that 37% of Welsh emigrants were women in the second half of the 19th century, they are often hardly visible.

Once again the figures are revealing in showing regional differences within Wales: for every county the figures for female emigration are lower than for male emigration, but sometimes the divergence is substantial. In general, for those predominantly rural counties where the emigrants tended to head for a rural area in the USA, they were more likely to go as a family group, and so the differences between the sexes are less marked. On the other hand, emigration from industrial counties was spearheaded by single men, who set off to exploit the better opportunities and higher wages available in American industry, and so the male emigration rate was substantially greater than the female emigration rate.

WHERE DID THEY GO, AND WHERE DID THEY END UP?

When trying to work out how many Welsh emigrants ended up in the different destinations around the world, there are many problems. As noted, the official records are not always trustworthy because the Welsh are under-represented: furthermore, so many migrants were mobile, adapting their plans as they responded to changing circumstances and economic developments. Having said that, the USA was clearly the prime destination for Welsh emigrants for almost every year in the 19th century – the exceptions being a few years in the early 1850s when the Australian Gold Rush was at its peak. Towards the end of the century both Canada and Australia were becoming ever more popular for Welsh migrants: it is likely that Canada was the most favoured destination in the first years of the 20th century.

'Welcome to Swansea'. Death Valley, California

Despite the impression you might get from certain accounts of Welsh emigration, Patagonia was never a prime draw, and indeed more Welsh emigrants went to South Africa than ever went to Argentina. (It is estimated that around 3,000 Welsh settled in '*Y Wladfa*', the Welsh settlement in the Chubut Valley, whereas in comparison there were over 4,300 Welsh-born residents of South Africa in the 1920s).

However, one very important aspect to bear in mind is that for many Welsh emigrants, their ultimate destination was home – Wales! It is estimated that between the 1870s and 1914, 40% of the emigrants from Wales and England returned home sooner or later – given the economic boom in the South Wales valleys in the latter part of this period, perhaps the Welsh figure is actually higher. This is an area where the official statistics are no help at all, so there is no sure way of knowing the exact percentage. However, if you look through the census returns for places like the Rhondda valley at the end of the 19th century you will find streets where there are numerous families where the eldest children were born in Wales, the middle ones born in America, and the youngest born in the Rhondda. (See, for example, the three such families in Miskin Street, Treherbert, in the 1881 census).

One of the consequences of this back-migration was that it helped to make the culture of these places reflect that of America in many ways: it was cosmopolitan, outward-looking and confident. There were many communities in Wales in the 19th century where what was happening in the USA was of just as much interest as what was happening in London, so that when you read the contemporary newspapers you find that their window on the world looked west across the Atlantic rather than east towards England.

16

WAS WALES BETTER BEHAVED IN THE GOOD OLD DAYS?

Andy Croll

Are standards of morality in Wales on the decline? A study of recent events on Barry Island would suggest they are. In June 2010, the *Western Mail* reported that it had become necessary for police to launch a 'dedicated campaign' on the island. The campaign was needed to tackle the anti-social behaviour that was undermining the resort's family-friendly image. During summer weekends, officers were to target drunks and confiscate their alcohol.

Barry Island – a busy Whitmore Bay beach in 1977

The crackdown (dubbed the 'Battle of Barry Island' by one newspaper) follows a period in which examples of drink-fuelled anti-social behaviour had apparently increased. Windows had been smashed at the Tourist Information Centre and gangs of 'sozzled' youngsters, some aged only 14, sat on walls intimidating visitors. In 2007, one thirsty youth arrived by train carrying a dustbin full of ice and cans of lager.

It was all too much for one Barry resident who complained she had found the beach covered with 'litter, pop bottles, cartons from fish and chips and every other bit of rubbish you could hope to find'. Why, she asked, 'can't these people have some respect for the lovely beaches they are spoiling and also for the people who come to the beach after them?'

Good question. What is it about some people today that makes them so disrespectful? Even more worrying is the feeling that the anti-social behaviour on Barry Island is just a symptom of a wider malaise gripping society. Behavioural standards, it seems, are on the decline. The campaign of 'zero-tolerance' on the Island was certainly born out of a sense of impending crisis. Things just weren't like this in the past.

GOLDEN AGES

The idea of a recent past that is morally superior to our own demoralised present is well entrenched in contemporary culture. 'Victorian values', for example, are often invoked as a shorthand reference to a 'better' time now regrettably passed.

It is true that Victorian Wales can seem an especially virtuous place. Just look at all the chapels they built. Think about the religious revivals they experienced. Wonder at a culture that encouraged miners to spend their evenings educating themselves (and lots of them did) in Institutes that they paid for and built themselves. Be impressed by a people who, in 1881, passed an Act of Parliament that closed pubs on Sundays as a mark of respect to chapel-goers. Compare and contrast the sexually chaste Victorian Welsh with today's over-sexed culture in which 'glamour' models are lauded as role models, padded bras are sold to seven-year-old girls and pole-dancing is marketed as a good way for young women to keep fit.

But the Victorians aren't the only ones who appear to outclass us in matters of morality. Pick any decade from the first half of the 20th century and the chances are they'll seem morally superior to any of those that come after the 1950s. We might disagree about the reasons for our fall from grace. Some will highlight the decline of organised religion; others will lament the ending of National Service; yet more will rue the day we did away with hanging and birching. Whatever arguments we might have about the causes of our predicament, common sense tells us that people in the past were better behaved and more respectful than today's loutish generation. If the past is a foreign country, it can frequently seem a more moral one too.

A DISORDERLY PAST

But is this true? Were things really so much better in bygone times? Consider another newspaper report of unseemly goings-on at Barry Island. One more dismayed resident of Barry felt moved to write to his local paper after witnessing some anti-social behaviour at Whitmore Bay.

'Bank Holiday crowds,' he began, 'must be allowed a certain amount of latitude, but surely certain sections of the holiday makers at Barry Island on Whit-Monday overstepped the mark.' This overstepping of the mark included 'several cases of drunkenness' as early as eleven o'clock in the morning, bottle-throwing and 'insulting behaviour'. Much to his dismay, 'the offenders were by no means all visitors'. The behaviour of 'several parties of youths (and young girls, too) did not tend to create a favourable impression,' he thundered.

This particular phase of the 'Battle on Barry Island', with its all-too-familiar scenes of binge-drinking and yobbishness, took place in 1925.

There are plenty more examples of loutish and inappropriate behaviour to be found in the newspaper archives. Littering was clearly enough of a problem in the 1930s to prompt one Barry school child to declare 'I do not like Barry Island very much because the sand gets full of dirty papers, banana skins and orange peel.'

Dirty behaviour of a rather different kind troubled respectable visitors to the Island at various points in the 1920s and 1930s. Police officers received 'numerous complaints' from picnicking families who were disturbed by strange men peering at them through hedges. The voyeurs were evidently hoping to see courting couples in various states of undress. The 'peeping Toms' were castigated for making a nuisance of themselves whilst the young couples' behaviour was described as being 'often disgraceful'.

We can go back further and still find examples of anti-social behaviour such as this – and worse. Thus, in September 1915 a Pontypridd collier was discovered exposing himself with 'the intent to insult females' on the beach. One outraged witness angrily told him he should be 'thrown into the tide'. Instead, he was thrown, less dramatically, into a local police cell.

Then there was the 'shameful deception by youths' which saw them enter

Butlins, Barry Island

the choppy waters of Whitmore Bay on a June afternoon in 1913. One of their number pretended to be drowning whilst his friends called frantically for the boatman who was paid by the council to patrol the bay. The boatman wasted a lot of energy in his pointless rescue attempt prompting an irritated local journalist to conclude that 'practical joking would be more suitable elsewhere'.

And lest it be thought that we could expect better from late Victorian visitors to the beach, consider the complaints made in the early 1890s about the louts who threw glass bottles from the cliff tops down onto the beach. A local councillor witnessed some of the bottles shattering at the feet of respectable visitors who were sitting on the sands. Unsurprisingly, 'he thought that these disgraceful proceedings should be put a stop to'.

CHANGING TOLERANCE LEVELS

Where does all this leave us in our efforts to wrestle with the question of whether standards of behaviour today are worse than they used to be? One important conclusion to draw is that there is little new about anti-social behaviour *per se*.

That is not to diminish the seriousness of any current examples of loutishness that blight the lives of many citizens today. But it is to say we should pause before declaring that 'it wasn't like that in our day'.

For we might not have behaved like 'that' whenever 'our day' was, but that doesn't mean that someone, somewhere wasn't behaving badly. Sometimes very badly. Sadly, late-Victorian South Wales newspapers contain a disturbing number of reports of serious sexual assaults of all kinds – even against children. Such appalling crimes are far from being an invention of recent years.

Does this mean that we are dealing with a history of morality in which nothing changes? Not at all. If we were to wake up in Victorian Wales we would be confronted with a moral landscape that could seem quite alien to us. To take just one example, the age of consent was only raised to 16 in 1885. Before then, sexual intercourse with a 13-year-old was deemed perfectly legal. Different eras draw the battle lines between acceptable and unacceptable behaviour in ways that are peculiar to them.

True, some patterns of anti-social behaviour are apparently unchanging across the decades. Drunken visitors to Barry Island, litter louts, disrespectful children challenging authority figures – these are issues of social concern today as much as they were in the late 19th century. However, we need to recognise how a different historical context might lead to seemingly identical instances of bad behaviour being understood in slightly different ways.

Take the racing of motor cars around public streets. In July 1914, Barry Islanders were suddenly plagued with car owners driving furiously on their roads. At first glance, this looks like another example of cultural continuity – joy-riders are still with us today, after all. But we would do well to dwell on the details.

Under the headline 'Islanders flee for safety', the *Barry Dock News* reported how a number of pedestrians scattered to safety 'to avoid being knocked down' by the driver of a motor car who was later charged with being a 'danger to the public'. It was clearly not an isolated incident for the next week it transpired that residents had sent in a petition to Barry Council protesting against the reckless driving of motor cars. Later that month, yet another report appeared of two cars 'racing' at Barry Island forcing several people on the road at the time to run for safety.

In all the cases mentioned, the speed demons were travelling at between 18 and 20 miles per hour.

These incidents remind us of the importance of historical context in defining what is, or is not, anti-social behaviour. 'Speeding' is a relative concept. Most right-minded people in 1914, the 'moral majority' if you like, simply could not tolerate cars travelling at 20 miles an hour in close proximity to pedestrians. Motor cars were still a novelty on the streets of South Wales at the time, and it was by no means obvious that they would (or even should) become the ubiquitous means of transport that they are today. As the magistrate remarked in one of the cases, 'There has been a great deal too much motor driving about.'

And before we congratulate ourselves on being so much braver and more worldly-wise than our not too distant ancestors, we would do well to ponder the wisdom of our tolerance of many more cars travelling at much higher speeds. For one of the consequences of our easiness with the automobile is an annual death toll on our roads measured in the thousands. We don't necessarily always know better than our forefathers.

This idea of ever-changing tolerance levels is key to approaching the history of anti-social behaviour. 'Anti-social' is not a natural, unchanging category. It is socially constructed. In other words, we decide what's anti-social or not – and we do so continually, arguing among ourselves, and often altering our views as we get older. 'Anti-social behaviours' change over time.

INDECENT EXPOSURE

Let's take another example from Barry Island's history to illustrate this point: changing attitudes to beach attire. We are used to thinking of the Victorians and Edwardians as being buttoned-up, quite literally, when it came to clothing. Stories of Victorians covering table legs in case they caused offence might be apocryphal but they nicely capture the prudishness that is frequently thought to characterise the period.

Certainly, one thing that becomes clear from even the briefest study of bathing habits in the late 19th and early 20th centuries is that many contemporaries were seriously concerned by the idea – and the reality – of too much exposed flesh.

Today, no one thinks twice of walking onto the sands at Barry Island, changing discreetly into a swimming costume on the beach and splashing around in the waters. Contemporary mores allow women to wear bikinis that expose arms, legs and midriffs. For men, of course, shorts will suffice – exposing even more skin both to the sun and the gaze of onlookers.

If our predecessors of a hundred years ago behaved in such a way they would have caused a riot. Photographs of Edwardian beach goers are remarkable to our eyes because of the dress code that was so carefully followed.

Sir, – I see young women going about with bare legs and bare arms. This shows that they are bare also inside their craniums. What if a man walked down Holton-road with bare arms – he would be run in.

'A Confirmed Bachelor'
in the *Barry and District News*, May 26, 1933

Indeed, for most visitors to Whitmore Bay there was little or no concession to the fact that they were spending a day on sand. Men in three-piece suits abound; women in their best dresses and bonnets are pictured picking their way cautiously over the uneven beach surface; even their children are shown trussed up in their everyday clothes.

Of course, if a man walked across the beach at Barry Island this August Bank Holiday in a suit and tie he would turn heads – for the wrong reasons. All of which is to say that fashions in beachwear change. But it is precisely out of this process of change that arguments about what constitutes acceptable and unacceptable behaviour are generated.

This is most clearly revealed in the history of naked bathing. 'Naturism' took off – so to speak – in the interwar period. But the idea that it was acceptable to take one's clothes off for bathing has a much longer history. It was thought perfectly normal for the most respectable of male bathers in the early 19th century to indulge in nude bathing.

By the later Victorian decades attitudes began to change. Local authorities passed bye-laws that defined, often in great detail, what bathing habits were and were not acceptable. Barry Island's beach by-laws were passed in the 1890s and had the effect of dividing the beach up into different zones. Women were to bathe in one half of the beach, men the other. There were rules governing precisely when bathing was allowed and what sort of clothes were to be worn. Nude bathing was most definitely banned.

But this was just one definition of anti-social behaviour. Some male bathers, in line with older ideas of what was acceptable behaviour, continued to run naked in and out of the waves in defiance of the by-laws. Their nudity upset many of their fellow beach users. However, tellingly, others seem to have delighted in the spectacle of the nude male form. More than once, Barry newspapers wrote disapprovingly of the young ladies who gathered on the nearby rocks, 'eyeing the men' as they bathed.

> On the bank overlooking the eastern end of the beach scores of ladies were seated... apparently having no other or nobler object than admiring the garbless forms of their lords. Such conduct on the part of the sex indicative of gentleness and refinement is, to my mind, truly deplorable.
>
> 'An Old Inhabitant' in the *Barry Herald*, July 4, 1902

CONCLUSION

What are we to conclude from the controversies aroused by the nude bathers, litter louts, 'peeping Toms' and speed demons from Barry Island's past? They certainly disallow any simple statement about 'the good old days' being morally superior to our own times. They might not have called it 'anti-social behaviour' but our predecessors from the late Victorian period through to the 1950s and beyond definitely had more than their fair share of trouble-makers, by-law breakers and reprobates.

Can we say anything meaningful about whether or not we are living through a period of moral decline? Not easily. It might feel like we are sometimes, especially when bombarded with an endless supply of media stories of crime, viciousness and immorality. But late Victorians often felt that they were living in particularly demoralised times. 'Jack the Ripper' did little to ease their fears on the point.

Whether moral standards are worse today than they were in the past is arguable. That they are different is certain.

THE IMMORALITY OF DANCING IN THE 1920s

There are serious moral objections to dancing itself... Dancing to-day brings about a closer contact of the sexes. So far as I am concerned the Zulus dance in a far more refined way than we do in civilised England and Wales... Modern dancing halls constitute a grave peril.

A Nonconformist Minister worries about the goings-on at 'Bindles' dance hall, Cold Knap, Barry. *Barry and District News*, March 16, 1928

17

WAS 1906 THE WELSH LIBERALS' FINEST HOUR?

Russell Deacon

The Liberals went into the election of 1906 under the banner of 'freedom'. Their slogan was 'Free Trade, Free Labour, Free Schools and Free Churches'. What the election would be most remembered for, however, was providing the first 'Tory free Wales'. As the Liberals secured so many seats in Wales and elsewhere, it is unsurprising therefore that this election soon became commonly known as the 'Liberal landslide'. Across the rest of the United Kingdom the Conservative defeat was also momentous but nowhere was it seen to be as total as in Wales. The events leading to the 1906 General Election result had been shaped by a series of stormy political events and unpopular polices on trade and education that led to Arthur Balfour's Conservative government becoming one of the most unpopular governments of all time.

A young David Lloyd George

Just as the Liberals were becoming united over a number of causes, such as free trade, so the Conservatives became divided by it. Winston Churchill crossed the floor to join the Liberals over this very issue, as did his cousin Sir Ivor Churchill Guest, the next Liberal MP for Cardiff. By December 1905, Prime Minister Arthur Balfour felt unable to continue to hold the Conservative party together and resigned. This led to the Liberal leader, Henry Campbell Bannerman, forming a minority government. For Wales this meant that leading Liberals David Lloyd George and Reginald McKenna (North Monmouthshire MP) were brought into the Cabinet. Lloyd George did not, however, become Minister for Wales as some had hoped. Instead he became Chairman of the Board of Trade. He was the first native Welshman to go into the Cabinet since Cornewall Lewis 50 years before in 1855. McKenna became Financial Secretary to the Treasury. With the new Liberal minority government formed, a general election was soon called.

Although across the United Kingdom and Ireland, the election lasted from January 12 until February 8, in Wales it finished on January 27. The last member to be elected was 46-year-old Liberal, John Herbert Lewis, for Flintshire. The first to be returned, was Sir Brynmor Jones, for Swansea District on the very first day of the election. Jones had no other candidate standing against him so was returned unopposed.

During the campaign some of the highlights of the election included torchlight parades and rallies, and the addressing of the huge crowds by prominent Liberals. Winston Churchill addressed a large Liberal crowd from the balcony of the Angel Hotel in Cardiff as he came to support his cousin Ivor Churchill Guest.

Just as the 1906 General Election was apparently dreadful for the Welsh Conservatives, it was beneficial for Labour in Wales. This was only the second election for the Labour Party and the first in its modern form. In 1900 it had returned two MPs, one of whom was Keir Hardie. Ironically the other Labour MP was Merthyr Tydfil-born Richard Bell, who won a seat also in the two-member constituency of Derby. Hardie had been helped in Merthyr Tydfil, Wales's only two-member constituency, by the Liberal mine and shipping owner D.A. Lewis. Thomas had become so disenchanted with the lacklustre performance of his fellow Liberal, Pritchard Morgan, due to his numerous absences from the seat and his broken promises, that he soundly backed Hardie instead, aiding his victory. Thus it was the Liberals that helped Labour into its first Welsh election win, a fact that would in time come back to haunt them, as both parties turned into bitter political enemies.

The scale of Liberal electoral victory across Wales was substantial in a number of seats. Aided by rejection of an unpopular government in the Welsh constituencies, the Liberal majorities rose considerably and for some MPs, such as David Lloyd George, it meant achieving a safe majority of 1224 votes (23.4%) over his Conservative opponent (R.A. Naylor) for the first time since they had entered Westminster (1892). In only a handful of seats were Liberal majorities now less than 10 per cent. In addition there were 12 unopposed Liberal or Lib-Lab seats in Wales. This represented almost half of the total unopposed Liberal seats for the whole UK.

THE RESULTS OF THE 1906 GENERAL ELECTION IN WALES

Party	MPs elected	Votes	Percentage of the vote	Percentage of the seats won
Liberal	28	103495	49	82
Lib-Lab	4	17569	8	12
Independent Labour Party	1	4841	2	3
Labour	1	10187	5	3
Conservative	0	70765	33	0
Liberal Unionist	0	2960	1	0

THE CANDIDATES

The candidates, in the days before salaried MPs, tended to be mainly self-supporting men of considerable private means. It was mainly their own money and resources that were put into the local campaign. The oldest MP to be elected was 65-year-old Sir Alfred Davies (Glamorgan East), whilst the youngest, Ivor Churchill Guest, was 32 years his junior. Guest was also one of the wealthier Welsh MPs and a number of his fellow Liberals were also wealthy businessmen, who controlled multi-million pound business empires. These included David Davies (Montgomeryshire – railways and coal), D.A. Thomas (Merthyr Tydfil – coal and shipping), and Lewis Haslam (Monmouth District – textiles). An indication of Haslam's wealth was that his estate was

Keir Hardie

valued at over half a million pounds when he died in 1922. To put this wealth into the context of 1906, a surgeon earned around £270, a policeman around £70 per year and an agricultural labour around £45. Lewis Haslam's personal wealth alone was around two thousand times that of an average surgeon, and over ten thousand times that of an agricultural labourer's annual income.

It wasn't only between the MPs and their voters that there was a huge social gap, there was just as massive a distance between some of the MPs elected as well. Labour's Keir Hardie, for instance, had worked since he was seven years old and enjoyed virtually no formal education

138

at all, a story reflected in most of the Lib-Lab MPs who came from mining backgrounds. The majority of the Liberal MPs, however, had attended English public schools and universities and then gone into business or the law. Of the universities they had been to, ten had been to either Oxford or Cambridge universities, five to London University with just two having a Welsh university education, at Aberystwyth. One Liberal MP who had not been to private school or university would trump all of his wealthier and privileged contemporaries. This was David Lloyd George, born in Manchester but brought up in North Wales, who already dominated Liberal politics in Wales like no other politician before or since. He would soon do the same in the rest of Britain.

FACTS ABOUT THE 1906 GENERAL ELECTION IN WALES

Date: January 14–27 (before modern communications systems, general elections would normally be held over the period of a month).

Electorate: 365,434 (only around 30 % of the Welsh adult population was eligible to vote, amongst those excluded were all women, and those males under the age of 21)

Turnout: 82.9 %

Number of Liberal MPs elected unopposed: 10 (29 % of all Welsh MPs)

Number of Lib-Lab MPs elected unopposed: 2 (6 % of all Welsh MPs)

Number of contested Welsh seats: 22 (65 % of all Welsh seats)

Largest constituency: Cardiff 26,475 voters

Smallest constituency: Montgomeryshire boroughs 3,304 voters

WAS THE LIBERAL VICTORY THEREFORE WORTHY OF THE NAME LANDSLIDE?

The Liberal victory was merely a fiction.

If you look back at the election statistics of the time and also project a short period into the future from 1906 you could say that the landslide was built on Welsh sand rather than Welsh slate. There were already plenty of signs that this was not the victory that many Liberals thought it would be:

- With only around 30 % of the Welsh electorate eligible to vote (all women were excluded), it can hardly be said this election result represented the true views of the Welsh population.
- The Conservatives were in a weak divided state and were unable to contest a third of the Welsh seats. This gave a false picture of strength to the Liberals.
- Already the Liberals had been defeated in many of the urban councils across Wales. In Swansea, Cardiff and Merthyr Tydfil, Liberals had all been defeated at a local level never to return in a large enough number to run the councils by themselves again.

- Although they won 82 % of the Welsh seats, the Liberals still failed to gain more than half of the Welsh vote.
- The Labour Party was still in its formative stages and worked closely with the Liberals. By the time of the next election they would be split and become fiercely competitive rivals. If Labour had been stronger in 1906 then the Liberal victory may not have been as solid.
- The election of David Lloyd George and his promotion into the government was a double-edged sword. Although he united the Liberal Party behind him in 1906, within a decade he would help split it in two ensuring that they would never return to government as a united party again.
- Even though the Conservatives didn't gain a single seat, they still gained a third of the Welsh vote.
- Those MPs elected outside of Labour and the Lib-Labs came almost exclusively from middle-class or aristocratic backgrounds. This lack of working-class candidates would in time alienate the working-class voters from the Liberals and drive them into the hands of Labour.
- Within a decade the Liberal Party would be broken, Labour would dominate Wales from now on and Liberals would disappear across most of Wales for the rest of the century.
- The Liberals failed to bring in the much desired Home Rule (a Welsh Parliament) when they had the opportunity to do so. Wales would have to wait almost a century before it was able to have a much weaker form of legislature than that proposed even in 1906.

EIGHT ENLIGHTENING FACTS ABOUT THE 1906 ELECTION

1 Although the Conservatives gained a third of the votes in Wales they did not gain a single seat
2 The Liberals gained 82 % of the seats but on less than half of the vote
3 It did not lead to a new Liberal government, the old Conservative government had already been replaced by a new Liberal one in December 1905
4 No candidate lost their deposit because these weren't introduced until 1918
5 The election saw the first widespread use of the motor car for both gathering the voting boxes for the election count and for getting supporters to the voting stations.
6 Political parties, political colours were still not fixed and were often chosen on the basis of local tradition or the candidates, own preferences.
7 Welshmen also did well in gaining seats outside Wales. Nine Liberal Welshman gained seats in England, including the first graduate from Cardiff University to become an MP, George Hay Morgan (from Hay on Wye) elected in Truro, and Clifford John Cory, the Cardiff coal shipper, in St. Ives. He gained that seat unopposed. There was also one Labour Welshman, Richard Bell in Derby.
8 Keir Hardie was the only MP in Wales who did not take the Parliamentary whip of the Liberal government.

THE LIBERALS' 1906 VICTORY WAS INDEED HISTORIC

There is also plenty of evidence that 1906 was, however, an historic victory. With 98% of the Welsh MPs taking the Liberal whip in Westminster, this clearly was a substantial electoral victory unparalleled in Welsh history. The 1906 Liberal victory in Wales was important for a number of reasons:

Statue of Lloyd George in Caernarfon

- It brought Welsh politicians into the heart of government for the first time. One of whom, David Lloyd George, would be the first and only Welsh-speaking Prime Minister.
- It established in the eyes of Westminster and the wider world that there was indeed a distinctive Welsh political voice that needed to be heard.
- It paved the way for later Welsh political and administrative devolution by accepting that Wales was indeed a distinct nation
- It put the Welsh Liberals in a dominant political position which would take it almost two decades to lose.
- The Welsh Liberals, particularly Lloyd George, took on directly the power of the aristocracy in the form of the House of Lords. Within five years the Liberals would have proved that the voice and will of the democratically elected members of Parliament would forever be more important than the unelected peers.
- It heralded the start of one of the greatest reforming governments in British political history. Over the next four years, through his People's Budget, David Lloyd George as Chancellor was able to introduce amongst other things pensions and sickness insurance. The extent and nature of these social reforms can still be seen today.
- Although the Liberals became the second party in Wales politically after Labour in 1922, it wouldn't be until 1951 that the Conservatives became the second party of Welsh politics.

141

THE FUTURE

Whether or not this was the Liberal victory it was made out to be, it did have a lasting effect on those who were elected. Over the next decade many of those Liberal MPs elected would find themselves at the heart of government. David Lloyd George and Reginald McKenna were already in the Cabinet. Others such as D.A. Thomas would follow. Henry Hadyn Jones, MP for Meirionnydd, who was elected in 1910, noted in the *Western Mail* in 1934 'that every member who was returned for a Welsh constituency at the memorable general election of 1906, would from now on be given a special bonus in the form of a peerage, a Privy Councillorship, a knighthood, a county-court judgeship, legal preferment in the way of briefs at the hands of the Treasury, or a place in the government' before the end of their career. The strangest thing perhaps about this election was that it was fought in a strongly partisan nature against the Conservatives. Yet within a decade many of these Welsh Liberals would join with the Conservatives in a coalition government under Lloyd George that would forever end the 'Golden Age' of Liberal Wales.

18

THE RIOTS OF 1910 – WHY DO WE REMEMBER ONLY TONYPANDY?

Louise Miskell

For many people in Wales, an outbreak of rioting in the Rhondda town of Tonypandy in 1910 is one of the defining moments in modern Welsh history. The riot has been fictionalised in Lewis Jones's novel *Cwmardy*. The website 'Welsh Icons' lists it as one of the historical events most representative of 'Wales and all things Welsh'. Local government and community groups in Rhondda Cynon Taf organised a series of events to mark the centenary of the riot in November 2010 with a programme of activities ranging from a heritage trail to a lantern parade through the town's streets.

The reasons for the important place occupied by the Tonypandy riot in our memories of coalfield history are not hard to find. For a brief interlude in early November 1910, normality was turned on its head in the mid-Rhondda town. Violence and looting spilled out onto the streets resulting in the widespread destruction of shops and property. The riot sent a high-voltage charge of fear through Edwardian society and led to the deployment of police and military reinforcements to quell the disturbances. In particular, the role of Winston Churchill, then Home Secretary, in determining the level of force to deploy in Tonypandy, has led to much myth-making, inaccurately characterising him as the 'enemy of the

Sir Winston Churchill in 1911

miners' and the man who 'sent the troops in'. It makes for a compelling story of honest Welsh colliers betrayed by a hostile government. It is not surprising that both professional historians and the public have found Tonypandy such a source of fascination.

But to remember Tonypandy is to remember only a fragment of a long and bitter industrial dispute which extended across much of the South Wales coalfield. The South Wales 'coal war', as it was reported in *The Times* and the *Western Mail* of the day, consisted of eleven months of strikes and stoppages spread across the Rhondda, Cynon, Garw and Afan valleys, where different sets of grievances led to a series of strikes and stoppages involving well over 20,000 mineworkers.

The bulk of the strikers worked for one of two colliery companies: the Cambrian Coal Trust in the Rhondda valley, and the Powell Duffryn Company in the Aberdare valley. At the heart of both disputes was the determination of the miners to resist the attempts of the colliery companies to protect their profit margins in the face of ever rising costs of mining coal in the geologically challenging conditions of the South Wales coalfield. Miners demanded that a day's labour in a difficult seam which yielded little, should be rewarded with a fair wage, just as a day worked in a more productive part of the colliery. In effect, the disputes were about securing a minimum level of wage.

Although there were similarities in their grievances, the Cambrian Combine and Powell Duffryn miners went about things very differently. The Rhondda men held a ballot and 12,000 of them went on strike officially at the end of October 1910, after giving the statutory one month's notice. The Powell Duffryn stoppage began on October 20, when workers at Lower Duffryn pit downed tools. Theirs was an unofficial stoppage. They received no strike pay and consequently the ensuing hardship cut deep into the community.

Superficially, their stoppage was a protest against the decision of the mine manager, E.M. Hann, to end the 40-year-old custom whereby miners were permitted to take home blocks of waste timber from the mines for use as household fuel. More broadly it was a reaction to the perceived threat to their livelihoods posed by the colliery company's drive to increase productivity. The workmen marched to neighbouring Powell Duffryn collieries at Aberaman and Cwmbach, and very quickly a stoppage involving some 8,000 Cynon Valley miners was underway. The 'Block Strike' as it became known locally, was every bit as violent as the Cambrian Combine dispute. Some of the key incidents of disorder were played out in late October and early November, at almost the same time as the outbreak of rioting in Tonypandy and yet, compared with events in the Rhondda, this has been all but forgotten. Only one or two historians have paid it any serious attention and there is limited public awareness outside the locality in question.

For large sections of the press covering the events in South Wales in the winter of 1910, it was the Aberdare dispute which was regarded as the more dangerous and aggressive conflict. Numerous disturbances broke out involving not just striking miners, but members of the wider community as attempts were made to enforce conformity to the strike. On November 2, some two weeks into their stoppage, striking workers attacked the houses of a number of minor Powell Duffryn colliery officials in Glamorgan Street and James Street, Aberdare. Suspected strike-breakers were hunted down and attacked by crowds of protesters, including large numbers of women who, in at least one case, 'stripped a man of his coat and waistcoat.' Elsewhere on the same evening, a train carrying some 90 to 100 workmen was attacked at the Tonllwyd crossing in Aberdare. Protesters smashed the train windows and pulled men out on to the platform while others fled the scene, pursued by 'a hooting crowd which grew in number as it went along.'

It seems likely that news of what was happening over the hills in the Rhondda valley spurred the Powell Duffryn men on. *The Times* correspondent, reporting from Cardiff, suggested that there was a ripple effect. The day after the Tonypandy riot, 'as though envious of their comrades in the Rhondda Valley', Powell Duffryn strikers marched to Cwmbach and attempted to attack the power station and adjoining wash-house at Middle Duffryn Colliery. The incident had clear echoes of the attack on the Glamorgan Colliery power station at Llwynypia the previous day.

At Cwmbach a small contingent of 29 police succeeded in repelling the strikers and their supporters by electrifying the perimeter fence and soaking the approaching crowd with hot water from the boilers. This incident alone resulted in some sixty injuries. One participant, Wil Jon Edwards, later recalled that the disturbance culminated in a police baton charge which forced most of the protesters, bruised and bleeding, into the muddy shallows of the adjacent canal.

The reputation of the Powell Duffryn strikers as radical and determined was further bolstered by the character of their leader, Charles Butt Stanton. Stanton was the Aberaman-born miners' agent who became the talisman of the Aberdare miners. As early as April 1910 he was singled out as the only miners' leader in South Wales to have refused to sign a new wage agreement with the coal owners (although he later relented). His most controversial act during the dispute, however, was his utterance of a supposed 'death threat' to E. M. Hann, general manager of the Powell Duffryn company. The threat,

Police on parade at Tonypandy

left in a telephone message on October 29, was widely quoted in the local and national press. Stanton was reputed to have said of the strike, 'if there is going to be any "black-legging" over this there is going to be murder. My God, I mean it.' In a mass meeting the next day on the Plough Tip, Aberdare, Stanton claimed that he had not meant to direct a specific threat to Hann, but rather to convey a general fear for 'what would happen if work proceeded on any large scale during the strike'.

The incident, though controversial, seemed to do nothing to diminish Stanton's popularity with the majority of Cynon Valley miners. When he stood up to speak at a mass meeting at the Market Hall, Aberdare, on November 1, he was greeted with a chorus of 'For he's a jolly good fellow'. More moderate speakers who tried to counsel against the spread of the strike were heckled and shouted down. There is some evidence to suggest that Hann didn't really take Stanton's 'death threat' seriously. At a meeting with magistrates, military and police commanders on November 11, he passed up an opportunity to ask for a police presence at his own home, but overall the number of police he requested to keep order at the Powell Duffryn collieries greatly outnumbered the corresponding requests made by Mr Llewellyn on behalf of the Cambrian Trust mines in the Rhondda.

Not surprisingly, the colliery districts of both valleys were filled with police reinforcements throughout the autumn of 1910. The streets of the Aberdare district in particular, echoed to the sound of horses' hooves, as mounted deployments conducted daily patrols up and down the valley, which was regarded as more suitable for the horses than the narrow, cobbled, tram-lined streets of Llwynypia. Detachments of troops, likewise, were stationed around the disturbed districts, including a company of the Loyal North Lancashire regiment, stationed at Aberaman. Part of the challenge for the authorities of the day was to co-ordinate police and troop movements over such a wide area with more than one centre of unrest. Tonypandy was just one likely trouble spot. Aberaman was another.

Given the seriousness with which the Powell Duffryn strike disturbances were viewed in the winter of 1910, it seems odd that it is now Tonypandy that gets all of the attention. Why has the Tonypandy riot come to overshadow the other elements of the 'Coal War' to such an extent? There are a number of possible explanations. First among these, perhaps, is our tendency to distil our past down to a number of convenient and familiar reference points. Thus the South Wales coalfield becomes the Rhondda, the 'Coal War' becomes the Cambrian Combine dispute, and the epicentre of unrest becomes Tonypandy. Historical memory is all about convenience, and the Tonypandy riot has become a convenient symbol of coalfield unrest in Edwardian Wales.

The Glamorgan Colliery strikers

A second explanation lies in our preference for satisfactory outcomes. The association of Tonypandy with the Cambrian Combine dispute meant that it has been seen as part of a more successful strike movement. The Cambrian men held out until September 1911. Their dispute had some identifiable legacies, notably in the publication the following year of *The Miners Next Step*, and the emergence in the leadership of the South Wales Miners' Federation of some of the prominent figures from the dispute like Noah Ablett.

In contrast, the Powell Duffryn men returned to work on January 2, 1911, with little immediate reward to show for their protest. They failed to persuade miners in the neighbouring valleys to join forces with them, or to cajole the Executive Committee of the Miners' Federation to endorse their unofficial strike action. Relief payments when they came, were too little and too late, and the heavy police and military presence in the valley had an intimidating effect both on striking miners and on the community at large.

While Tonypandy could plausibly be remembered as part of a proud tradition of labour history in the South Wales valleys, the Powell Duffryn dispute could not. In many ways, the figure of Charles Butt Stanton lay at the heart of the problem. If he was a controversial figure during the strike, this was nothing compared to his reputation thereafter. During the First World War, Stanton recast himself, shedding his role as radical left-wing miners' leader and becoming a jingoistic MP of the right. He stood against his former allies in the Independent Labour Party, most famously defeating ILP candidate, James Winstone, to win the Merthyr Boroughs by-election following the death of KeirHardie in 1915. For a while he rode successfully on a tide of pro-war euphoria. But later, when the anti-German hype of the war years gave way to horror at the scale of the slaughter, Stanton found himself consigned to the political and historical wilderness. With him, perhaps, went the 'Block Strike'.

TIMELINE (1910–12)

October 20, 2010: Walkout at Lower Duffryn Colliery and beginning of Powell Duffryn strike

October 29: Stanton's 'death threat' left in a telephone message to E.M. Hann

October 31: Beginning of official stoppage by employees of the Cambrian Combine mines

November 2: Riot at Aberaman. Colliers' train attacked.

November 8: Riot at Tonypandy. Churchill gives authority to General Macready to move troops into the disturbed districts if needed

November 9: Powell Duffryn strikers attack Middle Duffryn power station at Cwmbach

January 2, 1911: Powell Duffryn men return to work

Sepember 1911: Cambrian Combine strike ends

February 1912: Publication of *The Miners' Next Step*

As we read this essay, written exactly one hundred years after the Tonypandy riots, it is worth reflecting on what we choose to remember. The history that we decide to write about, talk about, televise or commemorate says as much about our own tastes and preferences as it does about the past. There is nothing remarkable about this. Bestowing special significance on particular events and giving them a more prominent place in the long-term historical record is of course an entirely practical, indeed essential, way of getting to grips with our past. We cannot recall every aspect of our history in all of its minute and complex detail. But, occasionally, it is helpful to look beyond the parts which we have carefully parcelled up for preservation for a glimpse of what lies beyond. The history we commemorate might just look a little different as a result.

19

DID WALES GO WILLINGLY TO THE FIRST WORLD WAR?

Robin Barlow

Welsh historians, and historians of Wales, have all largely concurred with the prevailing view that the people of Wales wholeheartedly supported Britain's entry into the war. The dominant images of August 1914 are of cheering crowds in town centres and on station platforms, long lines of men patiently waiting outside recruiting offices and soldiers marching away happily singing 'It's a long way to Tipperary'. Folk memory is a powerful factor, but are these images historically accurate?

It is, of course, impossible to talk about a Welsh response to the outbreak of war. There were differences between North and South Wales, between rural and urban areas and Welsh-speaking and non Welsh-speaking areas. However, historians have tended to generalize. K.O. Morgan has given the lead, referring to how the people of Wales 'threw themselves into the war with gusto', and pointing to 'heights of hysteria rarely matched in other parts of the United Kingdom'. He talks of 'jingo fever' and argues that the 'wholehearted support that Welshmen of all parties and creeds gave to the war itself', was in 'striking contrast to the divisions of the recent past'. J. Graham Jones talks of a miraculous display of 'vigour and enthusiasm' for the war and a 'patriotic frenzy' and D. Gareth Evans refers to 'patriotic fervour pervading the land'. Well, where is the evidence for these sweeping generalisations?

THE OUTBREAK OF WAR

In Wales, in the early summer of 1914, there was certainly no expectation of war. On Bank Holiday Monday, August 3, 1914, 50,000 day-trippers descended on Barry Island to watch and listen to a grand band competition on Nell's Point, to picnic on the grass or to stroll on the beach. Similar scenes were witnessed throughout Wales whether in Mumbles, Aberystwyth, Llandudno or Tenby.

Welshmen are lovers of peace but they are defenders of liberty.

David Lloyd George

When war was declared on the following day, the vast majority of the population of Wales was unable to comprehend the reasons for this course of action, knew very little of the government's diplomatic policies and certainly had no perception of the nature of the war that was to come. The South African War was the only point of comparison: war was remote, fought by a professional army and would have little or no impact on everyday life in Wales. Lilly Powell, aged 12 at the outbreak of war, remembered, 'I'd gone down to Morriston to get the evening paper and there were crowds everywhere and all sorts of hullabaloo and I asked my friend what all the fuss was about and she said, "Have you been asleep or something? WAR has been declared!" '

Dai Dan Evans, like all miners, had been expecting a three-day Bank Holiday break from the pit:

> Nobody expected the war to come, I mean from little villages. Obviously the people that were in Parliament and people that were studying politics knew the trends and knew that there was something in the offing. But to the ordinary man in the street and to the children and teenagers, particularly, it would never dawn on them. So when the First World War was declared it was a shattering blow, see. It came like a bolt from the blue.

The 'patriotic frenzy' and 'heights of hysteria' referred to earlier, seem even more unlikely against the backdrop of the broadly liberal, Nonconformist and pacifist tradition of Wales. In the 19th century, the regular army was seen as a refuge for the destitute and desperate, and for those who were unemployable in any other occupation. The *Welsh Outlook* commented, 'Our fathers believed that war under any circumstance was unjustifiable, and they looked askance at any young man who enlisted'. Ioan Gruffydd, writing of Anglesey, thought that the few who joined the army were regarded as social outcasts, 'having chosen the life to escape from the responsibility of living respectably'. Robert Graves observed that,

Lloyd George with Haig, Joffré and D.A. Thomas

151

'The chapels held soldiering to be sinful and in Merioneth the chapels had the last word'. The ranks of the army were overwhelmingly English, working-class and at least nominally Anglican. In 1913, Welshmen made up only 1.8% of the regular army, compared to 78.6% from England, 7.6% from Scotland and 9.1% from Ireland.

MANPOWER

- At the outbreak of war, Britain's army numbered 250,000, approximately one third of which was in India at the time
- In contrast, Austro-Hungary could call on three million men, France four million. Germany four-and-a-half million, and Russia nearly six million men
- By the end of the War, Britain's army had multiplied fourteen-fold and totalled nearly three-and-a-half million men
- 272,924 men from Wales enlisted in the British army, of which 122,995 were volunteers
- 12 % of all those from Britain who fought in the war died or were killed
- There were 16,500 conscientious objectors to the war, of which it is estimated 1,000 were Welsh

VOLUNTARY RECRUITMENT

The standard 'evidence' cited by most Welsh historians for a generally enthusiastic response to the outbreak of war has tended to rest squarely on one piece of evidence: the number of volunteers who came forward to enlist. But is this necessarily logical? What of all those who volunteered for all sorts of other reasons? Motives for enlistment were many and varied – a desire for adventure, to escape the mines or the fields, to break free from a constricting society or most importantly, because of economic necessity. The outbreak of war brought about an immediate economic depression which threw many men out of work and others on to short-time working.

When miner, B.L. Coombes, enlisted, he did so, glad to escape the 'machine roars and long hours' of the pit. Irving Jones of the 10th Battalion, Welsh Regiment was also working in a colliery: 'My brother-in-law and me, we discussed it and we decided to join up. We thought, well, a holiday maybe, you know, that's what we thought. We'd beat the Germans in about six months. That's what we thought'.

Oh yes, a great patriot I was, bloody glad to get out of the pit. I thought we would have a good time, have a good adventure, it was supposed to be over by Christmas...'

Oliver Powell from Tredegar

The statistical question, of just how many men from Wales served in the armed forces, especially in comparison to England, Scotland and Ireland, has proved to be a thorny issue for historians. The evidence for the army, however, is unequivocal, although frequently misquoted and misrepresented. Between the outbreak of war and

November 11, 1918, 272,924 men from Wales (including Monmouthshire) enlisted in the British army. Using estimates of the total population in July 1914, official statistics calculated that 11.57% of England's total population enlisted, compared to 11.50% of Scotland's total population, and 10.96% of Wales's population. When the figures for voluntary enlistment are examined, a similar picture emerges: 6.6% of Scotland's estimated population in July 1914 voluntarily enlisted, compared to 6.04% for England, and 5.83% for Wales.

The crucial factor about all these statistics is that Wales lags consistently behind both England and Scotland in all aspects of enlistment. However, countless historians, notably led by K.O. Morgan, have mistakenly reversed this league table, putting Wales ahead of England and Scotland, and consequently concluded that the vast majority of people in Wales gave

Members of the Monmouthshire Regiment

their full and wholehearted support to the First World War. The cause of this error is a reliance on the recruitment figures given by Sir Auckland Geddes, the Director General of Recruiting, in January 1918, and quoted in a book published in 1919 entitled *Wales; Its part in the War*. The figures were only estimates, did not cover the whole period of the war and thus have no value whatsoever.

TOTAL ENLISTMENT **1914-18**

Country	Total enlistments from all sources to 11 Nov 1918	Estimated total pop in July, 1914	Percentage of total pop represented by enlistments	Estimated male pop in July, 1914	Percentage of male pop represented by enlistments
ENGLAND	4,006,158	34,618,346	11.57	16,681,181	24.02
SCOTLAND	557,618	4,849,500	11.50	2,351,843	23.71
WALES	272,924	2,489,202	10.96	1,268,284	21.52
IRELAND	134,202	4,374,500	3.07	2,184,193	6.14
Total	4,970,902	46,331,548	10.73	22,485,501	22.11

[Source: *Statistics of the Military Effort of the British Empire during the Great War*, London, HMSO, 1922]

THE WELSH SOLDIER?

One further factor which must be taken into account when trying to assess whether the willingness of men to volunteer is evidence of broad Welsh support for the war, is who exactly was volunteering. Put simply, were the volunteers from Wales actually Welsh? According to the census of 1911, there were significant numbers of migrants to the very Welsh counties which were at the forefront of voluntary enlistment. In Glamorgan, 17.30% of the county's population had been born in England, whilst in Monmouthshire the figure was 22.40%. This is not to say that some Welshmen had migrated to England and would join up there, but nothing like the numbers which would have been travelling in the other direction.

If we look briefly at the volunteers to the Rhondda Battalions of the Welsh Regiment, we find further evidence of the dilution of the Welsh character of the units. Of those who had died between August 1914 and December 1916 (and would therefore almost certainly have been volunteers), we find that in 10th Battalion, Welsh Regiment (1st Rhondda Battalion), 18.4% had been born in England. The figure for the 13th Battalion, Welsh Regiment (2nd Rhondda Battalion) was that 21.1% were born in England. So now we have frequently misquoted, inaccurate statistics, with the added possibility that around 20% of the Welsh volunteers were actually English.

THE CALL TO ARMS

The statistics of voluntary recruitment clearly show that in Wales, as in Scotland, there was not the 'rush to the colours' that has often been portrayed. It was only in the final week of August 1914 that the number of recruits reached over 500 per day in Wales, with the main peak occurring in the first ten days of September. The most productive day for the Recruiting Sergeants in Wales was September 3, 1914, with over 2,000 recruits. By the end of the month this figure had soon fallen to an average of only 250 per day. The three Recruiting Districts in Wales produced only 2,000 recruits in total for the month of December 1914.

There were immediate concerns that Wales was not doing her bit for the war effort. In October 1914, Major Delme Davies-Evans of the Pembrokeshire Yeomanry, wrote to virtually every daily and weekly newspaper in South Wales appealing to the young men of the agricultural districts to enlist. After a week trying to get recruits, he wrote, 'the response has been most disheartening, 70% of the recruits are English boys, who have been working on Welsh farms'.

In North Wales, recruitment in the Welsh-speaking areas was consistently lower than in the English-speaking areas. In August 1914, one recruiter complained that 'ten days yielded but the paltry total of sixty men for Kitchener's Army in Caernarfonshire,' whilst another complained that 'no one registered in the regular Army in Anglesey during the last week of September'. Ellis W. Davies, MP for Eifion (Caernarfon), maintained that there was 'a deep feeling ingrained in the people against militarism'.

This evidence hardly points to wholehearted support for the war, jingoistic fever and a patriotic frenzy as has been claimed. Support was localised, not universal.

RECRUITING TACTICS

During the latter months of 1914, and into 1915, those responsible for recruitment tried everything they could to boost the numbers of volunteers from Wales. On April 5, 1915, a parade was organized through the streets of Cardiff, involving 5,000 schoolchildren who had fathers or brothers fighting in the armed forces. A banner held by one child read, 'My Daddy is at the front, what is yours doing?'

Sporting events were seen to be an effective way of reaching potential volunteers. On April 17, an international rugby union match was organized by the military authorities at Cardiff Arms Park, between a Welsh XV and an International XV, drawn mainly from England and Scotland. Nearly all those who played had previously been capped by their respective countries; nine of the Welsh team and all those in the combined team were members of the armed forces. Successfully combining the two religions of Wales was the pack leader Rev. Lieutenant Alban Davies, chaplain to the 6th Battalion, Welsh Regiment. Recruiting sergeants were on duty throughout the game and anyone who enlisted on the day was given free admission. Prior to the match, the crowd was entertained

'Come with me, boys!
Join up today'

by the bands of the 3rd Battalion, Welsh Regiment and the Queen's Own Cameron Highlanders, whilst at half-time 'stirring appeals were made to the spectators to join the forces'. Despite all these efforts only 58 volunteers came forward on the day.

In early May 1915 the 3rd Battalion, Welsh Regiment despairingly sent a recruiting party to Manchester. Over 500 recruits were obtained in one week, necessitating a special train being commissioned to bring the men to Wales. This was followed by a procession through the streets of Cardiff, headed by a banner proclaiming, 'See what Manchester did in one week for the Welsh Regiment. Now, Cardiff, what will you do?'

On May 22, a boxing carnival was held at Cardiff Arms Park, attracting a crowd of 8,000, which included both military bouts and professional exhibition contests. The top billing was a 20-round bout between Driver Joe Johns (Merthyr) and Arthur Evans (Tir-phil) for the Welsh lightweight championship, fittingly won by the military man. Only 38 volunteers came forward during the day.

A SOLDIER'S LIFE

Given the conditions under which many recruits had to live, it is perhaps surprising that anyone volunteered at all. A recruit from Llanelli, who had enlisted in the town with the Royal Field Artillery was sent to Shorncliffe. Clearly this army did not march on its stomach: breakfast was one-sixth of a loaf of bread, lunch was potatoes and stewed meat, and tea was a repeat of breakfast. Knives and forks were scarce, and meals were eaten using only fingers; this was matched by those who served up the meals, as the orderly who served the potatoes used, 'his hands only in the process'. Reveille was at 5.30am. with parade at 6am., followed by a swim in the sea and a four- or five-mile march, all before breakfast. No uniforms or kit were issued, and the men had only the clothes they stood up in, and consequently lice and vermin were rampant in the tents in which the recruits were living.

A.E. Perriman joined the South Wales Borderers and was sent to the Regimental Headquarters in Brecon:

> The washing facilities and toiletry were disgusting. There was no hot water available. On each floor was a two-handled tank of considerable proportions which was filled, or thereabouts, during the night by barrack room occupants. In the morning it had to be carried away and emptied by a room orderly with the help of a volunteer. Reveille at 6 a.m. followed with beating of drum and blaring bugle in the barrack rooms made further sleep impossible. Breakfast consisted of a pint size basin of tea, undrinkable because of grease from

The Battle of the Somme

previous meals, floating on top, which almost turned one's stomach, chunks of bread, pieces of margarine and fat bacon.

WALES AND THE WAR

Although it has been shown that Wales contributed proportionately fewer recruits to the British army than either England or Scotland, this is not to denigrate the part played by many Welshmen. Whether at Gallipoli, Mametz Wood or elsewhere on the Western Front, there are numerous tales of individual bravery and heroism. However, away from Glamorgan and Monmouthshire – especially in rural, Welsh-speaking areas – there was not the support for 'England's army' or 'England's war' and certainly no jingoistic fever or patriotic frenzy.

THE WELSH ARMY CORPS

- The WAC came into being as a result of a speech made by David Lloyd George at the Queen's Hall, London on September 19, 1914
- The Corps had its own distinctive uniform made of homespun brethyn llwyd
- Lord Kitchener (Secretary of State for War) said that no purely Welsh regiment was to be trusted, and that they were 'always wild and insubordinate'
- When recruiting for the WAC officially ended in October 1915, 50,000 men had volunteered, forming the basis of the 38th (Welsh) Division

20

HOW CLOSELY KNIT WERE OUR FAMILIES AND COMMUNITIES?

Stephanie Ward

One question that often intrigues us about history is 'How different was life in another period?' How did people think and feel, what did it look like and how did the past smell and sound? Above all we often wonder whether people were happier. Part of the draw of the popular *Coal House* series on the BBC was this interest in daily life in the 1920s. Could we see what people ate, wore and did for fun? Similar questions intrigue historians too, and especially the wider issues they can raise about Welsh society. Whilst measuring the happiness of people is impossible, historians can at least investigate the day-to-day lives of Welsh people. One way of examining these particular issues is to look at the age-old customs of love, courtship, marriage and family life. In the 21st century we often decry the current state of society and apparent breakdown of family and community life. It is perhaps natural to assume that there was a 'golden age' of family and that 'things were better back then'. But how much of these ideas are a comforting blanket of nostalgia, and how much is based upon reality?

MARRIAGE AND FAMILY IN EARLY 20th CENTURY WALES

At the end of First World War the marriage rate in Wales soared in line with the rest of Britain. In 1920 nearly 26,000 couples married, signifying optimism at the end of the Great War and of reunited couples and demobbed soldiers. A similar position existed at the end of the Second World War when the number marrying again increased. The family was central to community life, although it was transforming. By the interwar period the size of families in Wales had decreased to an average of three to four children per household. A decline in the birth rate, the wider availability of contraception and out-migration affected numbers. The depression of the 1930s clearly made an impact upon Welsh family life.

LOVE ON THE DOLE?

Black-and-white photographs and the shadow of the Great Depression leave the 1920s and 1930s often appearing as shades of grey. Indeed, with some of the highest unemployment figures ever recorded in Britain, perhaps this is unsurprising. While we may not question the importance of family within Wales, we can ask how could people fall in love and continue to have children amidst the grind of poverty and years without work? The simple answer is, of course, that life could not be put on hold forever and the world was not only grey. People wanted to continue on life's path. Or maybe the novelist Gwyn Thomas had it right when he noted that 'love, properly used, keeps people warm'.

There was great stigma attached to marrying whilst unemployed as immortalised in Walter Greenwood's classic 1933 novel *Love on the Dole*. The press decried beginning married life living on the state and taxpayers' money, and warned of the dangers of bringing children into a world without work. Surely without seeing parents work, the next generation would choose not to, an idea that has persisted. However, for young people marriage represented adulthood as much as entering work. It could also mark the end of employment for women either through choice or the practice of not employing married women. Before marriage, of course, came courtship and with it the mating rituals of the age.

The street was an important meeting place for young people in the 1920s and 1930s. Archie Lush in his social study of youths in South Wales noted that the habit of 'walking out' was most popular for cash-struck youths. It also offered plenty of opportunities for meeting the opposite sex through a custom known as the 'monkey parade'. On Friday and Saturday evenings and on Sunday after chapel, boys and girls would line the streets on opposite sides of the road. Girls would walk in twos or threes past a line of chatting young men hoping to catch an eye. Many hours were spent strutting in the monkey parade and it was denounced by the more zealous chapel deacons. If successful, courting couples would meet in cafes and cinemas, and the more daring would walk off into the dark of the mountain. For the young in Wales, courting continued, even if many delayed marriage until work was found and a home secured.

'*MYND I GNOCIO*' – 'GOING TO KNOCK'

In the countryside courting practices and opportunities for meeting potential suitors could take a quite different form. Again we can see the influence of economic considerations, where ensuring the financial survival of the family unit was a perennial priority. Sons of farmers married much later on and many never married at all because of inheritance patterns and the custom for fathers to set up a farm for sons upon marriage. There were also often fewer women as many had to move away for employment.

Girls in rural communities had fewer opportunities for socialising than their urban counterparts and would often meet young men when walking home from social occasions. A study carried out in Llanfihangel yng Ngwynfa in Powys in the 1940s by Alwyn D. Rees noted that the most common courting practice was for young couples to meet in the kitchen of the girl. The boy would get the girl's attention by throwing stones at her window, known as *mynd y gnocio* ('going to knock'). They would then meet in the kitchen until the early hours while her parents slept upstairs. Alwyn D. Rees noted how 'during vigils with the Home Guard in 1940, traffic came to an end about midnight, and one could rest until dawn when young men would be going home on their bicycles'. Such relationships would not be revealed in public until a formal proposal. Upon marriage, the couple would usually set up home in a new farm. Where this was not possible, different generations of families would temporarily live under the same roof.

THE FAMILY

Parents were greatly concerned about the morals of their children, and of their daughters especially. Such concern was often a direct result of the policing influence of neighbours and relatives. Failure to keep up appearances and maintain chapel-worthy morals could lead to ostracism from the community. Although it did undoubtedly happen, having sex outside marriage for girls was a sign of loose morals and it could reflect badly upon the whole family. This was especially true if it resulted in pregnancy and marriages had to be hastily arranged. Until the 1970s, many men and women remained virgins until marriage. Before the wider availability of the Pill from the late 1960s, fear of pregnancy made young women cautious about having sex.

Aside from their responsibility for their children's moral upkeep, parents also had a hold over them financially, albeit often unintentionally. As we have seen, in rural areas it could prevent adult sons from marrying. During the Depression in urban areas like South Wales, monetary burdens were as much a constraint as they were a separating influence. The introduction of the controversial 'Means Test' for the long-term unemployed had an adverse effect on many working-class households. The test required the household income to be pooled. In the worst case this meant that working sons and daughters could end up supporting their unemployed fathers. It was customary for

A model of family life in Ebbw Vale

working-class children to give the majority of their income to their parents. The difference the means test made was in enforcing this relationship and it prevented children from accruing any savings or money for themselves. The consequence of this system was to prevent sons in relationships being able to set up their own households. For fathers it was undoubtedly emasculating. Having a daughter become the main breadwinner turned the hierarchy of the family on its head.

The wider impact of the means test and the Depression was to cause families to split up. Adult children would usually remain at home until married. However, the compulsion to find work would lead sons and daughters to travel away to England. Daughters would take up employment as domestic servants in places like London or Liverpool, sending the small amounts earned through backbreaking labour to their parents. While some had positive experiences, tales of girls falling into prostitution or immoral ways flourished. Sons were attracted to places like Coventry and Slough for work in car factories. While the family unit was sacred, economic necessity did lead to the encouragement of children to migrate to more prosperous areas. For those who managed to obtain work locally, the place within the family could be no less secure.

Sons would take up lodgings elsewhere so fathers could claim a higher rate of unemployment benefit. Working children also spoke of wanting to leave home and its burdens. The separation of families for these reasons led to heavy criticism of the government for introducing a policy that led to the breakdown of family life. Chapel leaders were particularly vocal. It also led to the march of tens of thousands on the streets of South Wales in protest.

How many families separated during the Depression is difficult to measure. We need to be mindful of those sons who only pretended to move away to deceive means-test inspectors. There is enough evidence to suggest that contemporaries believed that this was happening. Even when a separation was temporary, it calls into question the idea that families struggled through together as a unit at whatever cost.

FOR BETTER FOR WORSE?

One of the most notable changes to the family unit in the post-war period has been the decline in marriage rates and the increase in the number of divorces. Such patterns reflect a number of important changes within Welsh society. They can tell us as much about a change in attitudes towards sex and relationships as they do of developments in technology, changing living standards and, of course, the Law. In 1921 there were 721 divorced people living in Wales. By 1971 the number had risen to 24,305.

The rise in the divorce rate suggests that families were more likely to split up in post-war Wales. However, as with all statistics we must be careful to question what they tell us. What is undoubtedly clear is that important changes to the divorce law had made it easier and brought it within the reach of the working class. In the interwar period, divorce was only an option for the middle and upper classes as it was an extremely costly affair. For those men and women, in particular, wishing to escape marriage, there was little choice other than to separate. With young children and few employment opportunities, this was often not an option for the majority of working-class wives. It would take a reform of legislation and the 1969 Divorce Act especially to free women from unhappy marriages. For some, divorce could be an extremely liberating experience. After divorcing a violent and abusive husband, Eva Goldsworthy recalled how 'that January afternoon I walked away from the law courts free. Free from the shackles of marriage, free from musty offices and the musty smell of law books. I stepped into the world like that advertisement for Startrite Shoes – a toddler walking up a path towards the sun. That was me at 45 years, setting out to be my own person'.

It was not only the costliness of divorce that served as a discouragement. Divorce carried a stigma, as did lone parenthood, well into the middle decades of the 20th century and even beyond. Women were shamed into staying as much as men were into taking responsibility for a child outside marriage. The loss of influence of the wider community in policing itself in this way has all but left most corners of Wales in the increasingly privatised world of the 20th century. Before legal reform and a revolution in attitudes, can we argue that couples were not more likely to stick together – they just had fewer opportunities to separate?

While marriage rates may have now reached an all-time low, wedlock remained extremely popular until the 1970s with couples marrying at a younger age. As affluence increased, many couples now met at the increasingly popular Saturday night dances taking place in larger towns across Wales. Gone were the days of the monkey parade and going to knock! Teenagers after the war experienced a sense of freedom and liberation denied to parents during the years of the Depression and wartime. Like marriage, family remained extremely important as indicated by the post-war baby boom. Indeed, many within Wales began to socialise as a family unit more than had previously been the case.

Battling to save a community, protesters object to the proposed closure of Llwynypia Hospital

New semi-detached council housing, the cheaper availability of cars and, perhaps above all else, the rise of television ownership meant that families spent more time together. Men would stay at home to watch popular TV shows on a Saturday evening rather than go to the pub. In this sense, families became more independent as well as private, taking car trips and holidays together as the standard of living rose.

From the 1970s, the family unit itself began to change. Although the majority of households (some 40%) in the 2001 census continued to take the form of a married couple and children, family life had clearly been transformed. Extended families of step-parents, half brothers and sisters, along with gay couples and lone-parent households, have increased. Such change in the family demonstrates the emancipation of women, a transformation in attitudes to sex and sexuality, as well as patterns of work and education. Some of these changes have brought unease about the position of family life and the future of Wales's children. Yet, if every generation has a dangerous youth culture to worry about, then it also has a loss of family life to mourn. This was as true of the 1930s as it is of today.

21

HAD WALES ANYTHING TO FEAR FROM THE COLD WAR?

Charlie Whitham

Between 1974 and 1995, the United States Navy operated a small and highly secretive base near the sleepy coastal hamlet of Brawdy, Pembrokeshire, that played a vital role in the Cold War. Officially an 'Oceanographic Observation Centre', United States Naval Facility (USNF) Brawdy was in fact the largest terminal in a worldwide network of undersea listening stations tracking Soviet submarine movements in the northern Atlantic. Though the 'secretive' American base was no secret to locals at the time, less well known is how central this little foreign base – so essential to the Cold War – was to the prosperity of the local community and how desperately locals and politicians, both Labour and Conservative, fought to have the military stationed there. Far from being a sleepy backwater, Wales, in hosting the Americans at Brawdy, was placed on the front line in waging the Cold War adding to the profound impact, both social and economic, that this troubled period had upon Wales.

MILITARY WITHDRAWAL

When the proposal to site the US Navy in Brawdy was announced in 1971, it was to great cheer. Pembrokeshire faced the prospect of a complete withdrawal of the British military from a region that had suffered shrinking military establishments since the end of World War Two. The economy of west Wales was, and still is, based almost entirely on the agriculture and services sectors, the latter deriving much of its sustenance from the military. A dwindling military presence in the area during the 1960s was capped in January 1969 when the region learned that the Royal Naval Air Service (RNAS), which had been based at Brawdy since the 1940s, was to be withdrawn as part of the Labour Government's intention to withdraw military forces 'east of Suez'. A political and economic storm erupted.

UNEMPLOYMENT FEARS

In preparation for the Government's cuts a special working group was organised in the Welsh Office and their report highlighted the importance of the RNAS base to the economy of the surrounding area. It was expected that none of those formally employed by the RNAS base would find further work because of the lack of opportunities nearby. As a result, unemployment in the Haverfordwest area would approach a staggering 15%, when in Fishguard it was 5.3% and in Milford Haven 10%. Pembrokeshire as a whole was already suffering in the late 1960s from an unemployment rate of 7.5%, three times higher than the UK average. A few days after this report the Labour government – helped by anxious calls from the Welsh Office and from local politicians – pledged publicly to give the 'highest priority' to finding a new defence role for the Brawdy airfield in view of the effect its closure would have upon the local economy. Peter Thomas, then Secretary of State for Wales, described the military's abandonment of Brawdy as 'little short of catastrophic', and feared that if a new military role was not

The old hangars at RAF Brawdy

found for the site, the local council representatives 'would be dealt a shattering blow and I might well be faced with resignations of important members of that body'. The MP for Pembrokeshire, Nicholas Edwards, whose Conservative Party in 1970 had replaced the Labour Party in government, immediately warned of the political consequences if a replacement defence task was not found for the area: 'In view of the importance of Brawdy [base] to the economy of west Wales, any uncertainty should be reduced to a minimum' or risk 'political suicide there'. In 1971 the Ministry of Defence (MoD) eventually found a limited defence role for Brawdy, but it was another three years before an RAF Search and Rescue squadron eventually moved in.

AMERICANS TO THE RESCUE

In a move that was more luck than design, the RAF commitment to Brawdy was to be augmented by the arrival of the United States Navy. Unbeknown to the Welsh Office and Westminster MP's, the MoD had been in secret talks with the Americans since 1968 over establishing an undersea listening station, and Brawdy came top of a list of potential sites in England, Scotland and Northern Ireland. At the end of 1970, a joint Anglo-American naval team chose Brawdy partly because it was 'welcome on political grounds as providing a further task in an area of high unemployment'. The MoD was also glad that it would be

The American presence at Brawdy

saved from spending additional funds purely 'in order to provide employment in Pembrokeshire' until the Search and Rescue unit arrived. The American base was indeed a bargain for the British, who were being asked to contribute just £1.5 million to the Americans' £80 million for a base that would supply intelligence only to the US and British militaries – not the rest of NATO. Still, the British bargained hard to avoid even this small financial commitment, and it was several months before an agreement was struck for the US facility to be built at Brawdy.

In the public announcement of the good news to the Haverfordwest Borough Council on November 12, 1971, MP Nicholas Edwards spoke of the arrival of hundreds of Americans who should make 'a very substantial contribution to the economy of the area'. The economic hole left by the RNAS was as good as filled. The American facility was erected next to the former RNAS base (newly designated RAF Brawdy) on land already owned by the MoD. The MoD acknowledged that the US base would be created 'in an area of outstanding natural beauty' as the Pembrokeshire Coast Path ran close to the site, but was confident that by the end of the operation 'we hope that nobody will even notice we have been there'.

EXCEPTIONAL COMMUNITY RELATIONS

Far from remaining invisible, once it became operational in 1974 the US base left an unforgettable imprint on its surroundings. USNF Brawdy was highly successful in developing a good rapport with the locals, being viewed by the Americans as a 'showcase' for community relations. Over the years USNF Brawdy personnel were involved in a variety of events raising thousands of pounds for local charities. They also collected clothing, cleaned up beaches, river beds and cemeteries, and purchased equipment for a local hospital. There was also a close relationship established between USNF Brawdy and Portfield Special School for disabled children in Haverfordwest, buying toys and equipment and organising parties. These local activities were capped in 1994 with the holding of a 'Special Olympics' inspired by the facility's head of security that engaged more than 150 base personnel.

PROTEST

This exemplary record of harmonious military-community relations was rarely challenged, although the highly secretive base inevitably attracted attention from political opponents of an American military presence on British soil. Although there is no evidence to suggest that nuclear material was ever

169

CND members keep vigil outside Brawdy in 1983

present at USNF Brawdy, the shroud of secrecy that enveloped the facility meant the Welsh 'Area 51' was the target of several anti-nuclear protests during the 1980s. The largest of these was a march by 'Women for Life on Earth' from Cardiff in 1982 that ended in the creation of a peace camp at the gates of the base for the four days that US President Ronald Reagan visited Britain. Fascination with what the base might be up to fed a series of reports of UFO sightings in the vicinity of Brawdy, which during the 1970s were so numerous that the British military entertained launching a discreet investigation into the stories. Not all believed the Americans were unwelcome: the local *Western Telegraph* condemned the protesters as unrepresentative of local feeling and for not recognising that USNF Brawdy was a member of a regional defence establishment that was 'a vital part of the economy of west Wales'.

HIGH ECONOMIC IMPACT

And it is in the realm of economics that the positive embrace of USNF Brawdy can best be explained. Even though by the standards of other US military installations in the UK it was a small base, for a variety of reasons USNF Brawdy had a tremendous impact upon the local economy. The base establishment quickly grew. By 1980, USNF Brawdy had reached a complement of 22 officers, 278 other ranks and seven civilian workers with an annual budget of $20 million.

Even though some food and material was flown in weekly, the contribution to the tiny local economy was sizeable. Even after the Cold War, in 1993 there was still a total of 375 naval personnel stationed at the American base along with 320 dependants, and a 'conservative estimate' put the base's local contribution at £1.8 million a year, which included £800,000 spent on diesel, spare parts, concrete and tools, and £162,000 on contract services such as cleaning and rubbish disposal. On top of this, the 190 families were calculated to spend around £750,000 a year in the locality, some 25% of their income. Roughly 80 American children attended local schools in Haverfordwest, Solva and St. Davids.

CLOSURE FEARS RETURN

Little wonder that when it was announced USNF Brawdy would close, heated debate resurfaced over the economic plight of the region in a manner similar to that of 1970–71. A campaign to save the economy of Brawdy was led by the *Western Telegraph* which helped the local Conservative MP Nick Ainger in his demands for immediate government help for the region and his push for urgent meetings with the Welsh Secretary, David Hunt, and Armed Forces Minister, Archie Hamilton. Ainger and the campaign to prevent the closure of the RAF base failed, and the squadron left in 1994 leaving behind a reduced contingent to service USNF Brawdy until it closed in 1995. Despite a renewed battle to prevent a complete military withdrawal, which campaigners argued 'would lead to vastly increased unemployment and would all but cripple the Pembrokeshire economy', the US base site was handed back to the MoD, and in the same month RAF Brawdy closed as the remaining personnel were no longer needed to service the US base.

As many had predicted, employment in the region suffered. Luckily, and in common with events of the early 1970s, the government finally came to its senses and found a replacement role for the withdrawn RAF and US Navy forces. In 1996 the former RAF site became home to around 400 members of the 14th Signal Regiment (Electronic Warfare). Once more, the military ensured Brawdy had a fresh economic lifeline.

LONG MILITARY TRADITION

USNF Brawdy plugged a hole in the area left by the Royal Navy and together with the RAF sustained the local economy. Though the US base was small, in relative terms it supplied a crucial economic lifeline in a region that lacked any sizeable economic opportunities. In west Wales this relationship with the military has a rich tradition that long predates the American visitation. Its coastal approaches, remoteness and low-density population made south-west Pembrokeshire an ideal base location and training ground for the British military, and for naval installations of all types for years. No fewer than 431 military sites are known to have existed in the county stretching from the 19th century. Much of this presence centred on Milford Haven and Pembroke Dock which owed their existence to Admiralty involvement that reached its peak during the two world wars. Pembroke also played host to twelve military airfields sited mostly along the coast, with the earliest dating from the First World War.

Indeed, the attraction of the region was not restricted to British forces. USNF Brawdy was in fact the latest incarnation of a long association of the US Navy with the Pembrokeshire area. In 1918 American destroyers were stationed at Pembroke Dock, and for six months in 1943 a US flying-boat squadron operated from the RAF base at the Dock. Meanwhile American soldiers trained on beaches at Amroth and Wiseman's Bridge as US engineers built the largest Advanced Amphibious Base of over 1,000 servicemen and women for the US Navy at Milford Haven in preparation for the Normandy landings in 1944. And those who witnessed the West German Army set-up camp in Castlemartin during the 1960s can testify to how the region played host to other NATO forces during the Cold War. Indeed, military expenditure in Wales increased along with elsewhere in the UK as the Cold War intensified in the early 1980s.

FIRING LINE

This overriding regional economic dependence on the military no doubt accounted for much of the cordiality between the locals and the Americans. These factors, coupled with the fortune of the secretive base to avoid the level of protest that more high-profile American bases in England endured (such as Greenham Common), enabled USNF Brawdy to foster a good rapport with its neighbours in what was an otherwise turbulent period in Anglo-American political relations.

Also, USNF Brawdy existed during a period of political 'calm' in the nationalist debate over the future direction of Wales, and it was not until after the base closed that nationalist arguments gained force in Welsh politics. This meant that broader questions, such as about the way in which decisions regarding national defence are made, were not seriously tested during USNF Brawdy's tenure. Hence the American presence was viewed – at least by the influential Welsh politicians, civil servants and it seems most of the locals – more in terms of its economic virtue than for its generation of any wider political discomfort. But larger political questions, such as the stationing of foreign forces in Wales or the place of military spending more widely in the Welsh economy, are definitely raised. Wales was placed in the firing line of Soviet missiles over a non-NATO facility agreed without consultation with Welsh political representatives or local authorities. There is no doubt that in the event of an attack from the east, as the key installation in an undersea listening array, USNF Brawdy and its peaceful rural hinterland would have been a prime target for Soviet missiles. In a nuclear exchange Wales therefore shared the fate of western Scotland (with its US nuclear submarine base at Holy Loch) and the numerous US airfields in south-east England. The fact that USNF Brawdy was a non-nuclear facility removed some of the anxiety about its presence, but the principle, nonetheless, of the manner in which the facility was agreed and the nature of its role in Britain's defence being kept away from Welsh consideration remains a subject for future generations to ponder.

22

WHAT PIECE OF WORK WAS RICHARD BURTON?

Chris Williams

Richard Burton ate only laver bread until he was five. From that point on he drank three bottles of vodka a day while making love, one at a time, to every famous and beautiful woman in the western world. All his films were critical flops and box-office disasters, but he had a great voice and, of course, he was Welsh!

Sounds familiar? Although almost all of what you have just read is a spoof (of course he did have a great voice and he *was* Welsh), it is written in the spirit of much of what passes for authoritative comment about Richard Burton, the Pontrhydyfen boy who became a stage and silver-screen phenomenon and a global celebrity.

Richard Burton

Despite some honourable exceptions (such as Peter Stead's *Richard Burton: So Much, So Little*) many biographies of Burton (and of Elizabeth Taylor) are badly researched and poorly written. They seek to capitalise on public interest in Burton by recycling and embellishing the many lurid, sensational and improbable stories about his private life (some of which, of course, he started himself).

Richard Burton's widow, Sally, deposited his papers at Swansea University in 2006. Since 2008 I, along with archivists Elisabeth Bennett and Katrina Legg, have been working on Richard's diaries, and they reveal a very different Burton from the one seemingly uppermost in the public mind.

THE DIARIES OF A PRIVATE MAN

It is probable that Richard Burton kept more diaries than those that have survived to be deposited in Swansea University. Perhaps in due course some may resurface. For the time being, there is plenty to work with.

We have diaries covering all or part of 15 years, starting with a schoolboy's pocket diary in November 1939 when the then Richard Jenkins was 14, and ending in April 1983, a little over a year before Richard's death at the age of 58. Some are handwritten, some are typed. Some are in bound volumes, some are loose-leaved, in folders or binders. Taken together there are almost 400,000 words covering 93 months of a very active and fascinating life.

Most of these words date from the years 1965 to 1972, when Richard was married to Elizabeth Taylor. As such they offer unrivalled insights into the thinking of Burton at the height of his powers, and into the passions and priorities of a surprisingly private man.

Why did Burton keep a diary? Probably not with the intention of publishing it in its raw state. Rather it was to act as an aide-memoire, a private record of his life, to which he intended to return at some future, unspecified date. Perhaps he thought of writing a memoir, an autobiography, but he is vague about this. Certainly he thought that writing was a good habit, a way of keeping, as he put it, 'my mind in some kind of untidy order'.

Why did he stop keeping a diary? Burton was happiest writing when his life was stable and he was in control, and when he was 'resting' between film or stage projects. When he was really busy with a film, he often found it difficult to write. When his personal life became really troubled, he perhaps couldn't face writing, and when he drank to excess he was not capable of writing. So there are frustrating absences in the record – nothing, for instance, when he returned to Wales early in 1971 to make *Under Milk Wood*; only a few entries at the beginning of rehearsals for what would be his and Elizabeth Taylor's best film together – *Who's Afraid of Virginia Woolf?*

Yet what we have is still substantial and immensely rewarding. Of course, no diarist can be assumed to be entirely truthful, even to themselves, but Burton's official biographer, Melvyn Bragg, who had access to some of these materials when writing his 1988 book *Rich*, felt that 'here [Burton] speaks as truthfully as he can'. Or, as the man himself put it in 1969: 'I never lie when I write. Honest. Though I'm not sure of that!'

The diaries reveal a very different Richard Burton from the one most familiar to the general public. We still find in their pages Richard Burton the acclaimed actor, the international film star, the jet-set celebrity, but we also find Richard Burton the family man, the father, the husband. They reveal the melancholic,

An extract from Richard Burton's diaries

afflicted, troubled and introspective Richard Burton struggling to come to terms with the missed opportunities and unfulfilled potential of his life and talent. They show us the Richard Burton justly proud of his achievements, of his journey, hungry to scale greater and more distant heights. In the diaries we have him watching his weight, watching his drinking, watching other men watching *his* Elizabeth. And we have a Richard Burton reading, thinking and writing.

THE VORACIOUS READER

Burton's reading habits were obsessive-compulsive. Often finding it difficult to get to sleep, he would read and read into the small hours. Not infrequently he read all day – one, two, three or more books. On December 30, 1968 he spent 16 hours reading Arthur Schlesinger's blockbuster *A Thousand Days: John F. Kennedy in the White House*. Four days later and he read a history of the *Daily News*, a 'Hornblower' novel by C. S. Forester, and H. E. Bates's *Fair Stood the Wind for France*.

Some of Burton's favourite presents were books, and he often lists them in his diaries. A biography of Trotsky arrives from director Joseph Losey in advance of *The Assassination of Trotsky* – 'days of splendid reading', writes

Burton. Elizabeth gives him the entire *Oxford English Dictionary* one year (actually three sets – one for their house in Mexico, one for their home in Switzerland and one for their yacht). And third wife Suzy has a portable bookcase made for him that he can take from hotel to hotel while performing in *Camelot* in 1980.

Burton delighted in raiding bookshops. For example, in September 1971 he was shooting *The Battle of Sutjeska* in Yugoslavia. Grabbing a few hours off, he found in Sarajevo a store with a good English-language selection. Deciding to build up the library on his yacht – the *Kalizma* – he buys 'a complete Shakespeare … complete Keats, Shelley, Wilfred Owen, Louis MacNeice, Wystan Auden … a Larousse English dictionary … and a fat Penguin paperback of *Ulysses*'.

Burton's literary tastes were extensive – Shakespeare, of course, but also poets such as John Donne, Henry Vaughan, T. S. Eliot and W. H. Auden, playwrights including Oscar Wilde, George Bernard Shaw, Noel Coward and Tennessee Williams. His favourite novelists included Charles Dickens, Anthony Trollope, Thomas Hardy, Evelyn Waugh and Graham Greene.

And that's just those writing in English, for Burton was an enthusiastic linguist who enjoyed trying to read literature in the original. He was most successful at French, throwing himself in the early 1970s into the works of Baudelaire, Mallarmé, Rimbaud, Proust, Balzac, Dumas and Stendhal. Gaining command of a language offered him access to a different culture and a new set of insights.

As a proud Welshman, reputed always to wear an item of red clothing (and to insist on taking St David's Day off as a holiday to be celebrated in style), Burton's passion for Welsh writing is well known. Dylan Thomas had been a personal friend whose work remained a great influence. He treasured the poetry of Alun Lewis. Gwyn Thomas's writing made him laugh. R. S. Thomas did not, but he was a 'true minor poet'.

Burton did not only read 'serious' literature such as one might find on a university curriculum, although he did plenty of that. He was addicted to adventure, detective and crime stories (his favourite authors included Georges Simenon and John Le Carré, who was a personal friend), and he loved writing about a wide variety of sports – baseball, cricket, football, golf and, of course, rugby.

What a stupendous God he was, he is. What chance combination of genes went to the making of that towering imagination, that brilliant gift of words, that staggering compassion, that understanding of all human frailty, that total absence of pomposity, that wit, that pun, that joy in words … It seems that he wrote everything worth writing.

Richard Burton writing in 1970 about William Shakespeare

He is a deeply educated and remarkably unself-conscious man. He combines education with intuition to an unusual degree. He is a brilliant actor (in fact, he is all actor), but he is also an enemy to vulgarity and a man at war with boredom.

The American actor William Redfield, writing about Burton in 1964

177

THE IDEALISTIC THINKER

Some of Richard Burton's reading helped him relax. Some helped him escape, dream, marvel at language and enjoy wit. But his diaries also reveal a man who thought deeply about the world – past, present and future.

Burton was addicted to history and historical biography, fascinated by leaders, statesmen and politicians. He read up on Wellington, Palmerston and Disraeli, on Queen Victoria, Lloyd George and Oswald Mosley. In preparing for film roles he studied Alexander the Great, Napoleon, and Mussolini, Trotsky, Tito and Churchill. Intrigued by contemporary politics, he read heavyweight tomes on American Presidents, on the Cuban Missile crisis, Chairman Mao and Josef Stalin.

Having lived through the Second World War, Burton devoured military, economic and diplomatic histories of that conflict. Travelling to southern Africa in 1975 he became 'engrossed' by African history and particularly by the history of the Zulu people. He ranged wider still – biographies of George Custer and J. B. S. Haldane, studies of the Holy Land and of the Mayan civilisation, of the creation of the Suez Canal and of the discovery of DNA.

Richard Burton was in search of 'what it all meant', but found little comfort in the lessons of history. 'I love the world', he wrote in 1970, 'but if I take it seriously I shall go mad.' He worried about the risks of nuclear war in the 'age of abyss' and showed a prescient concern for the environment, seeing humankind as 'the beautiful Earth's greatest enemy'.

Though he often projected a world-weary air, at the heart of Richard Burton's thinking was located an idealism, a humanitarian impulse that hoped for a world in which distinctions of class, race and colour would be eroded, in which privilege would succumb to merit. It was to his never-ending frustration that this ambitious objective seemed to be getting no closer. If anything, by the end of the 1960s, the forces of darkness appeared to be gathering. Burton's heroes – John F. Kennedy, Bobby Kennedy (both of whom he knew personally) and Martin Luther King – had all been assassinated. He had very little respect for those who came after them.

At times Burton despaired of seeing real progress, but if he was an idealist he was not an ideologist. He gave short shrift to religious faith of any kind, had no truck with totalitarianism, was dismissive of communism. In his admiration for the dissident voices of George Orwell, Albert Camus, Arthur Koestler and Alexander Solzhenitsyn we see a respect for honesty, at whatever price it came. He prized the individual conscience, freedom of thought, and the uncontrollability of human expression beyond anything else. He put his bruised faith in Sidney Webb's 'inevitability of gradualness'.

Richard Burton in the radio studio

When I first realized the scale of Richard Burton's engagement with not just the great poets and writers but also with modern history and contemporary politics, I began to wonder at the origins of his immense intellectual energy, and the purposes to which he hoped to put his knowledge and understanding.

A knowledge of the world and its literary treasures offered Richard Burton a standard other than that of the film industry by which to measure himself. He wanted to be his own man, a man of substance and not a man famed mainly for speaking and reading the words of others. But that is not the full story. Richard Burton was in search of more than simply a sense of self-worth. He aimed for a profound comprehension of the world he lived in. He genuinely wanted to understand the eternal values – of truth, of aesthetics – and the prospects for the human race. Literature, the humanities, he saw as windows onto the soul of mankind and he read the past for signs of the future.

Richard Burton made no secret of his ambition to write, more than that: to become a great writer. That never happened. But when his diaries are published they will restore some balance to our understanding of this most intriguing man. Let him, in his diary entry of July 12, 1971, written in Gstaad, have the last words: 'Heard … this morning that Julie Andrews is in town also that John Kenneth Galbraith has just left. Wish it were the other way round.'

23

DID WALES REALLY SWING IN THE SIXTIES?

Martin Johnes

The English poet Philip Larkin once wrote that sexual intercourse began in 1963, sometime between the end of the ban on the publication of *Lady Chatterley's Lover* and The Beatles' first LP. He wasn't being literal of course but was the 1960s when the Welsh woke up to sex too?

THE TIMES ARE A-CHANGING

They say if you remember the 1960s, you weren't there. Today the image of that deacde has become one of sex, drugs and rock'n'roll, a time when the young broke down the old moral barricades. But the reality of being young at the time was more complex than that. Many led rather ordinary lives, more characterized by watching television and drinking coffee than taking drugs and having sex. But there was a spirit of change in the air and everyone was aware than the times were 'a 'changing' as Bob Dylan put it.

It was pop music that encapsulated the spirit of change. By the 1970s it was big business and could be heard everywhere from cafes and pubs to churches and eisteddfodau. Groups like the Beatles and Rolling Stones inspired the young and infuriated the old with their volume, long hair and

The Sixties swinging at the Top Rank suite, Cardiff

lack of restraint. There was also something inherently sexual about them, and pop music was central to how the question of sex commandeered so much public attention in the sixties.

IF YOU TRY REALLY HARD AND YOU'RE NOT PARTICULAR
YOU USUALLY END UP ALRIGHT

It was inevitable that the spirit of challenging conventions would impact on matters of sexual behaviour. That began, in a public sense at least, with the publicity surrounding Penguin's publication of *Lady Chatterley's Lover* in 1960. On the one hand, it was a victory for freedom of expression but people were also shocked at how the young openly queued to buy this 'dirty' book. Swansea library purchased a copy but it was only available on request. Young female assistants were not allowed to handle it and older female staff were allowed to refuse to do so. Libraries in Cardiganshire refused to stock it at all.

Such shock got another public outing three years later with the Profumo scandal, where a government minister turned out to be having an affair with a young woman who had also slept with a Russian attaché. To some the scandal was funny or just further evidence of the hypocrisy of the upper class, but it also contributed to talk of a developing malaise in the nation's sexual morals.

Some of the young were quite happy to feed this and shock their elders by talking about sleeping around. One young Welshman told a television reporter in the mid-1960s about trying to pick up girls for sex at dances: 'If you try really hard and you're not particular you usually end up alright'. By the end of the decade this had grown into something of a philosophy. According to advocates of free love, sex was a natural urge and should not be confined by social conventions like marriage or even relationships. Extra-marital sex obviously ran contrary to chapel morality and some even thought that promiscuity was un-Welsh. Concerns about it lasted throughout the 1960s and yet no one was quite sure just how much sex was taking place outside (or indeed inside) marriage.

Marriage certainly remained at the heart of society and of most young people's expectations. The number of illegitimate births in Wales did rise from 1,683 in 1960 to 2,983 in 1969. But even this was still lower than the 3,261 illegitimate births in Wales in 1945. In 1969, the year of the so-called summer of love, 93% of Welsh births were legitimate.

A quick marriage following conception was the obvious reason why most births were legitimate but that was hardly a new solution. As early as the start of the 1950s, 69% of births to married Welsh mothers under twenty happened between zero and eight months after their marriage.

The fact that this happened meant there was a degree of realism about the question of premarital sex. In rural areas there was often some tolerance towards unmarried mothers too. This meant they did not feel they had to leave home to have their baby. They were still gossiped about and censured by the chapels, but one social scientist working in Llanfrothen argued that most people there did not generally regard premarital sex as wrong and even suggested that it was more common in rural areas than in towns.

NICE GIRLS DON'T

In the towns it was not uncommon for the authorities to try to prevent anything that might encourage sex outside marriage. Throughout the 1960s, sex education was not allowed in Swansea schools and the town's university refused to introduce mixed-sex halls of residence. Two medical officers at the university in Aberystwyth were sacked in the late 1960s for refusing to divulge to the college authorities the details of students who had become pregnant. Students' freedom was further curtailed by an 11 o'clock curfew in most halls of residence with harsh penalties for breaking it.

There were plenty of other things to discourage premarital sex too. The idea that 'nice girls don't' remained strong, at least partly because knowledge of biology and intercourse was often confused and rudimentary. This gave sex a rather naughty and frightening undertone for many young women. There were also practical difficulties that discouraged premarital sex. Simply finding somewhere to do it could be difficult and extramarital intercourse was invariably in cars or outside in places such as mountainsides or back alleys.

Then there was the question of contraception. The introduction of the pill in 1961 was never quite the revolution that popular memory makes out, at least not until the 1970s and 1980s. Some historians stress how difficult it could be for unmarried women to get the pill. Officially, it was not until 1967 that GPs would prescribe the pill to unmarried girls and even then most required some form of reassurance or proof of a commitment to marriage or at least a stable relationship. In practice, however, doctors' attitudes were more diverse and could be considerably more liberal. Some people even remember being given the pill when dressed in school uniform.

Perhaps more of a hindrance than the attitude of doctors was the fear of asking in the first place. Most young women were simply not as confident about sex as the media outcry of the time suggested. Part of that was being afraid of what people would say. When one Swansea mother found out that her engaged daughter was on the pill in the late 1960s, she did not speak to her for a week. It took a degree of courage and bravery for girls to risk such wrath and disapproval. Yet more and more girls did risk that, both because this was a time to challenge conventions and because some of their peers expected it of them.

By the end of the 1960s maybe 10% of women in Wales were on the pill. One of them remembered: 'You felt it was expected of you to have sexual relations on the first date really, and you felt you were damned if you didn't and damned if you did. And, in hindsight, rather than liberalising women and freeing them up, I think it entrapped them more.'

Despite the barriers, it does seem that premarital sex in stable relationships was on the up, even if promiscuity was the habit of a minority. A British survey suggested that at the end of the 1960s around a quarter of men and two-thirds or more of women were still virgins when they married. This either means that a lot of men were boasting or a third of unmarried women, and no doubt some wives too, were seeing to the needs of three-quarters of unmarried men.

The mixed attitudes of the young were clear in a series of articles run by the *Western Mail* in 1969. The paper interviewed young people from across Wales about their attitudes and found strong support for sex outside marriage but little evidence of rampant promiscuity. A 20-year-old student in Cardiff

In search of freedom, Lesbian and Gay march in Cardiff in 1985

spoke for many when she concluded, 'Now that the risk of unwanted children is virtually over, there is no reason for not having sex when you are single. But I don't believe in free love. Love becomes obliterated that way'. A RAF serviceman from Cardiganshire was blunter: 'Sex before marriage? Sure. The bird might be frigid. You don't want a bird that's no good in bed, do you?'

Not all the young men were so blatant. A 20-year-old farmer's son from Johnstown said, 'Sex before marriage is all right if you love the girl. If you don't, it's wrong. Romance means everything to me.' Some young people were also very traditional about marriage and a 20-year-old trainee teacher from Caernarfon told the reporter firmly 'If you have a conscience you won't go to bed with a fellow before marriage – however right the papers make it seem'. There was also evidence of both double standards and traditional worries. A 19-year-old female clerk from Pontypridd summed up, 'A boy is a hero if he goes to bed with a girl – but the girl is called a whore. It isn't easy to be virtuous today... The idea that all young people know all about sex is quite wrong. Many of my friends worry about the first night of marriage'.

FREAK OUT

Such evidence did not stop the Welsh press dwelling upon reports of venereal diseases to decry contemporary morals. VD statistics for Wales were first published in 1970 and they showed that the number of cases was 6,632, an increase of nearly 74% since 1966. This was a steep rise but it was still hardly a widespread problem.

The legalization of abortion in 1967 was another cause of much of the concern. Hospital abortion was actually possible before its legalization in 1967 if it was for mental or physical health reasons. In practice though, this often came down to whether a woman could afford to pay for the procedure. After its legalization, there is nothing to suggest that it was a cause of promiscuity. In 1970, of the 3,031 notified abortions in Wales, 1,765 were actually had by married women.

None of this is to say that some of the excesses of youth culture in the 1960s did not hit Wales. There were, after all, over 6,000 cases of VD in Wales in 1970. Even at the start of the 1960s there was, in Cardiff at least, something of a scene for art students with drugs, parties and a cafe on Queen Street full of 'loose schoolgirls looking for sexual adventures, petty thieves, quasi-intellectuals, young guys on the make as the well as the hip cool beatniks,' according to one regular. This scene remained hidden from most people's attention but by the end of the decade the press was writing about bands that covered the stages of clubs with flowers, took drugs and exhorted their audiences to 'freak out'.

The *Herald of Wales* described one concert: 'In the middle of the dance-floor some kissed while others kept their eyes fixed intently on the strangely-clothed group. One well-educated and half-naked boy wearing coloured beads and bangles told me that he saw nothing wrong in making love when and where he pleased. His girlfriend agreed.' Some of this audience saw flower power as a religion, others took drugs to find their true selves and dressed in beads and flowers to 'counteract the hard, tough reputation of the male'.

Drugs were gradually coming to replace sex as the major cause of concern, especially as rural Wales started to attract drug-users from England seeking to drop out from mainstream society. Whereas older people understood sex, the world of drugs was alien to them and thus more worrying. With the newspapers running stories about addictions and hallucinations, two teenagers who loved each other having sex just seemed less of a problem.

A QUIET REVOLUTION

For most people, the excesses of the Swinging Sixties were things that happened in the newspapers and on television. But the anxiety that sons and daughters might be behaving in such ways made the issue real and relevant.

Yet for most families the reality was more mundane than free love. A mother from Merthyr remembers the 1960s as 'screaming' rather than 'swinging', 'as I yelled at the family to cut down the volume on the transistor, screeched in despair as the Rolling Stones were played for the umpteenth time on the record player and squawked my head off at teenagers about getting their hair cut'.

Unmarried couples sleeping together or short skirts on teenage girls were no longer quite the scandals they had once been. That did not mean they were fully accepted by everyone, but gradually dominant attitudes were changing. There was what another writer in the *Western Mail* called, a 'quiet revolution' in morals.

That revolution may have started with teenagers, but it trickled upwards too, encouraging some older people to challenge received wisdoms and codes of behaviour, a process that was, of course, reinforced by the young themselves growing older. Perhaps the most important facet of this revolution was not the sex that preoccupied commentators but wider freedoms.

The questioning of conventions gradually gave people freedoms as diverse as drinking in pubs on Sundays, dressing how they wanted and using Welsh in their dealings with officialdom. One woman even wrote in the *Western Mail* in 1969 that changing manners meant that

Were they really permissive? No, of course not... All we did during the Sixties was discard our mock modesty... Let us look at them as a time when free speech became a little nearer being free and sex became the acknowledged way of conceiving babies.

The women's page of the *Western Mail* in 1970

Sleeping arrangements at Bardney Pop Festival, 1972

females could now ask others about the price of their dresses and 'use four-letter words in mixed company.' She did, however, warn that older men would still be shocked.

The middle-aged and elderly did indeed struggle to accept changing values. Thus one woman recalled being asked to leave a Cardiff pub in 1966 because her skirt was too short. Some pubs would not let women in at all. Such attitudes meant the revolution arrived more like a tortoise than a hare but it arrived all the same, bringing less deference and less acceptance of the status quo. That was what the Swinging Sixties really meant.

SOME KEY LANDMARKS IN THE SWINGING SIXTIES

   1960: Penguin found not guilty on obscenity charges for publishing *Lady Chatterley's Lover*
   1961: First referendum on Sunday opening of pubs in Wales. Five of the 13 counties vote in favour.
   1963: Profumo scandal
   1963: *Please Please Me*, first Beatles alum released
1965-6: Miniskirt becomes popular
   1965: John Rowlands's *Ienctid yw 'Mhechod* contains the first detailed description of sex in a Welsh-language novel
   1967: Legalization of abortion
   1967: Consensual sex between males aged 21+ legalized

24

WHAT DID THATCHER EVER DO FOR WALES?

Martin Johnes

In 2008 a row broke out about the display of a portrait of Margaret Thatcher at the Senedd. One Plaid Cymru AM called putting it there an 'insult to the people of Wales'. Mrs Thatcher probably invokes stronger feelings than any other political figure in history. But is the venom that is so often aimed towards her deserved?

THE ECONOMY

At the heart of the hatred of Thatcher lies her record on the economy. The Conservatives came to power at a time of significant economic problems and rising unemployment was one of the key reasons for her victory in the 1979 General Election. Yet those problems deepened after 1979, at least partly because government policy prioritized fighting inflation over unemployment.

In 1979, there were around 65,800 people unemployed in Wales. By 1990, the year Thatcher left office, there were 86,600. Those bare statistics disguise just how bad things had got in between. In 1986, there had been more than 166,000 people in Wales on the dole. By then less than 40% of Welsh households were headed by someone in full-time employment. Nearly a fifth of men out of work had been so for five years or more.

There were glimmers of hope. The service sector grew significantly, as it did everywhere. Wales had some success in attracting inward investment from overseas and began to develop a reputation as a location for manufacturers from the Far East. Over the period 1979 to 1989, Wales attracted, on average, 13% of the total overseas investment in the UK each year, despite only having about 5% of the British population. The M4 corridor and the north-east were the particular beneficiaries. Clwyd, once an unemployment blackspot after the closure of the main Shotton steelworks in 1980, enjoyed something of an economic miracle. Its GDP went from 15% below the Welsh average in 1981 to 11% above it in 1995.

The economy did recover after 1986 and unemployment halved in four years. This all brought much talk, from the media, politicians and academics, of a Welsh economic miracle based on modernization, diversification and attracting hi-tech investment. But such perspectives were rooted in just how bad things had got in the early 1980s. After that, even a small economic growth could seem remarkable.

Unemployment remained a significant problem and many of the jobs that had been created were part-time and unskilled. This, like the rise in the service sector, was important in bringing more women into the workforce. Indeed, the growth in female employment offered an important financial cushion to families where the man was out of work. By 1990 there were 55,000 more women in employment in Wales than there had been in 1979 but there were also 98,000 fewer men. The Welsh economy certainly changed during Thatcher's tenure as prime minister, but it is difficult to escape the conclusion that she left it weaker than she found it.

A police escort for Margaret Thatcher at City Hall, Cardiff in 1980

THE MINERS

Controlling the unions was a key reason for middle-class support for Thatcher. Yet, by some measures, the level of strikes actually increased after she took power. Thanks partly to a major steel dispute, more working days were lost in strikes in Wales in 1980 than in 1979, the year of the so-called Winter of Discontent.

It is, of course, the miners' strike of 1984–5 that marks Thatcher's relationship with the unions. Although badly led by Arthur Scargill, it is difficult not to sympathize with what those on strike went through. They endured more than a year without pay, were vilified by parts of the London media and were the victim of some fairly unjust and even brutal tactics at the hands of the authorities.

There are some today who like to say that the sympathy of Wales helped the miners survive and that the strike was an important moment in waking Wales up to its political neglect from London. That argument makes some sense and yet there were complaints at the time that other unions, the Labour Party and parts of the community were not doing what they could to help the miners. Moreover, the widespread sympathy that did exist for the miners was not really political but rather a compassionate concern for the suffering and impossible situation fellow Welsh people found themselves in.

The miners' defeat was a watershed in Welsh history but it was not quite the cataclysmic event that it is often portrayed as. The key decade for the decline of Welsh coal was not after 1984, when 22,000 jobs were lost, but the ten years after 1958 when 50,000 mining jobs went. By 1981, the proportion of Welsh employees working in mining and quarrying was just 3.8%. Mining had a symbolic importance but its economic importance to Wales as a whole had long since faded.

Nor was the strike the cause of the end of mining. The culprits there were oil and gas. Thatcher's government simply applied the final fatal blow to an industry that had long been in terminal decline, although that hardly excuses the relish with which it seemed to do it. The strike was, however, the last gasp of an old kind of politicized working-class solidarity. Never again would a trade union try or even contemplate taking on the whole state.

After the strike, the coal industry collapsed at frightening speed. There was plenty of coal left but little political will to exploit it. Twelve collieries closed in South Wales within 18 months of the dispute's end. The remaining pits were invested in, improving productivity and moving the coalfield into an operating profit in 1986 for the first time since 1958. But even then closures continued and substantial recent investments were written off in what seemed to be a vindictive retaliation by the government. Some miners even thought that management was taking bad decisions to show that a pit was unprofitable and thus make closure possible.

THE END OF COAL

By 1990, there were just six pits left in South Wales and less than 3,000 miners. When Thatcher had come to power there had been 27,000. On January 1, 1995, the British coal industry returned to private ownership. When the NCB had been created 48 years earlier, it owned 203 collieries in South Wales; when it was disbanded it had just two.

The impact on those communities who lost pits was devastating. Unlike when collieries closed in far greater numbers in earlier decades, there were now fewer alternative jobs to go to. Many miners simply dropped out of the labour market, encouraged by a welfare system that made it relatively easy to claim incapacity benefit. The effect was that in some districts the percentage of people registered as permanently sick nearly quadrupled between 1981 and 1991.

With high numbers of people out of work, there was a knock-on effect on local services, leading to talk of communities being decimated. There had actually been complaints of community disintegration, depopulation and marginalization in the valleys since the 1960s but now they seemed more serious. Yet surveys showed that people in the valleys felt they had a stronger sense of community than other parts of Wales. Moreover, they objected to their towns being stigmatized and labelled as places of poverty and no aspiration. For all the economic misery the closure of the mines inflicted, valleys communities proved resilient and they had not depended on coal alone for decades.

Indeed, the passing of deep mining brought mixed emotions. The valleys were now green again and few miners actually wanted to see their sons go underground. Miners had a love-hate relationship with their job, and in time some came to think that they were better off out of it.

CUTS

There has been much recent talk of the cuts of the 1980s but often not much understanding of what actually happened. Public spending was certainly under pressure but it is very misleading to talk of cuts across the board. Welsh Office spending on health and personal social services actually grew from £543m in 1979–80 to £1,502m in 1990–91. This was because of rising wages, higher staff numbers, new hospitals, health promotion programmes and far

Police and miners' wives in conflict during the Miners' Strike

more people using the service. Yet there was never enough money to go round and a constant strain on budgets marked the 1980s.

This was especially true of local government which seemed expected to bear the brunt of the pressure on the public purse. Local government spending cuts had actually begun under Labour in the late 1970s as James Callaghan's government shifted its priority from fighting unemployment to fighting inflation. From then onwards, councils struggled and were forced to cut back on maintenance and equipment for everything from local roads to schools. They also introduced new charges for some previously free social services provision. Across local government, there were redundancies and a general mood of gloom.

Many local authorities proved surprisingly resourceful in facing the challenges. Service delivery itself did not deteriorate drastically but the maintenance of the supporting infrastructure certainly did. This was something only too evident in the state of much council housing and the horror stories of crumbling schools in the local press.

It was in cuts to the welfare system where the real pain was felt. The government sought to reduce the value of benefits by removing various supplements and not always raising payments in line with inflation. Thus, at a time when average earnings were growing beyond inflation, unemployment benefit fell in real terms by 4% between 1978 and 1988, widening the gap between those in and out of work. In strict financial terms the changes may not have amounted to very much but they mattered to those who had to count every penny. Being 'on the social' was thus no picnic and it was the most vulnerable in society who suffered the worst when cuts were made.

A WELSH STATE

To compensate for the scale of economic upheaval that its policies were inflicting, the governments of 1979–97 enacted a number of changes that did much – indeed more than any previous administration – to buttress the official status of Wales and the Welsh language. After Gwynfor Evans threatened to starve himself to death, the government agreed to create a Welsh-language television channel. It also increased the subsidies to Welsh-language services and gave the language a place on every schoolchild's timetable. In 1993, after Thatcher had left office, Welsh was given equal legal status with English, leading to bilingualism becoming the norm on every sign and document produced by the public sector.

The powers of the Welsh Office were also extended and a host of new quangos were set up to monitor and govern Thatcher's free-market state. With quangos being appointed rather than elected, and control of the Welsh Office being decided by how England voted, none of this was at all democratic. But it did help modern Wales become a more defined nation than ever before. Indeed, under first Thatcher and then John Major, administrative devolution reached such proportions that it was not misleading to talk of the emergence of a Welsh state. The devolution of administrative power from London to Wales thus predated 1999. The National Assembly simply added democratic control to a devolution that had already happened.

The government got little credit for any of this. This was partly because there seemed to be little enthusiasm for it at the top. That these things happened at all owed much to ministers within the Welsh Office pushing hard against the instincts of the government's leading lights. In an argument with Welsh Office minister Wyn Roberts, Thatcher revealed some of her attitudes. Wales and Scotland, she thought, were holding England back. 'You have nothing! You contribute nothing!' she told Roberts before adding the 'only Conservatives in Wales are the English who moved in'. Roberts, quite rightly, objected, although there were many socialists who probably would have agreed with Thatcher on this last point.

THAT WOMAN

For all the hatred that was often aimed at Thatcher, some of her policies were very popular in Wales. Income tax cuts were welcomed by those in work. Few complained about the 140 new miles of Welsh motorway and trunk roads that were built between 1979 and 1990, or the 22 bypasses that alleviated Welsh towns of their traffic misery. Most popular was the right-to-buy scheme that by the end of 1991 had enabled nearly 84,000 council houses in Wales to be sold to their occupiers. Ultimately, the reduction in council houses fed house price inflation and reduced the availability of housing for those unable to afford to buy, but it did meet ordinary people's desire to enjoy the security and pride of owning their own home.

That policy helped win Thatcher support across Wales, including amongst members of the working class who had previously voted Labour. Although Labour clearly remained the most popular party in Wales, the knowledge that parts of the working class were voting Tory increased the anger felt by some who were suffering rather than benefiting from her policies. They may not have been rioting but Thatcher became hated in a way that no previous prime minister had. This was particularly evident during the miners' strike when Thatcher was venomously referred to as 'her', 'she' or 'that woman'.

Demonstrations at the Patti Pavilion, Swansea, greet Margaret Thatcher in 1980

A defiant striker in the arms of the police

Yet the majority of the Welsh people were not vehemently for or against most of Thatcher's specific policies. Only a minority voted for her but that does not mean there was extreme dissatisfaction with everything she was doing. Surveys showed that most people were neither particularly enthusiastic nor hostile towards the privatization schemes that were so important to Thatcher. Selling off the silver might not seem right in principle, but it was hard not to notice the improvement in some services after they were privatized.

What a majority of people did not like were the general principles that Thatcher seemed to represent. Thatcher was attacked for undermining the bonds of society by encouraging individualism and widening the wealth gap. Her retort was that she was creating opportunities and reducing dependency. The reality was that all those things happened to some degree and Thatcher's government brought about changes for better and for worse. Her problem in Wales was that even some people who benefited often did not recognize how she had helped, while everyone was aware of how she had not.

Indeed, the memory of her failures played its own part in persuading some doubters to vote 'Yes' in 1997. Thatcher would not like the label, but this made her one of the architects of Welsh devolution.

WALES AT THE POLLS

Tactical voting and the emergence of the Alliance complicate the picture but it is clear that a sizable proportion of the Welsh electorate supported the Conservatives and that the level of their support stayed fairly constant over the period.

	1979		1983		1987		1992	
	Votes	%	Votes	%	Votes	%	Votes	%
Con	526300	32	499300	31	501300	30	499700	29
Lab	768500	47	603900	38	765200	45	865700	50
Libs/SDP	173500	11	373400	23	304200	18	217500	12
Plaid	132500	8	125300	8	123600	7	154900	9

Notes on Contributors

 Robin Barlow is Higher Education Advisor, Recruitment & Admissions, at Aberystwyth University.

 H.V. Bowen is Professor of Modern History at Swansea University and Convener of History Research Wales.

 Janet Burton is Professor of Medieval History at University of Wales, Trinity Saint David.

 Andy Croll is Principal Lecturer in History at the University of Glamorgan.

 Russell Deacon is Professor of Welsh Governance and History at University of Wales Institute, Cardiff.

 Kathryn Ellis is Senior Lecturer in History at Glyndŵr University.

 Chris Evans is Professor of History at the University of Glamorgan.

 Madeleine Gray is Reader in History at University of Wales, Newport.

 Ray Howell is Reader in History and Historical Archaeology at University of Wales, Newport.

 Martin Johnes is Senior Lecturer in History at Swansea University.

Raimund Karl is Professor of Archaeology and Heritage at Bangor University.

Gethin Matthews is Lecturer in Welsh History at Cardiff University.

Louise Miskell is Senior Lecturer in History at Swansea University.

Katharine Olson is British Academy Postdoctoral Fellow in Medieval and Early Modern History.

Huw Pryce is Professor of Welsh History at Bangor University.

Karen Stöber, formerly of Aberystwyth University, now teaches at Universitat de Lleida in Spain.

Stephanie Ward is Lecturer in Modern Welsh History at Cardiff University.

Charlie Whitham is Senior Lecturer in Twentieth-Century United States History and Foreign Policy at University of Wales Institute, Cardiff.

Chris Williams is Professor of Welsh History at Swansea University.

Alun Withey is Lecturer in History at Swansea University.

Suggestions for Further Reading

M. Barclay, '"The Slaves of the Lamp": The Aberdare Miners' Strike 1910', *Llafur*, vol. 2 (1978)

Deirdre Beddoe, *Out of the Shadows: A History of Women in Twentieth Century Wales* (Cardiff, 2000)

H.V. Bowen (ed.), *Wales and the British Overseas Empire: Interactions and Influences, 1680-1830* (2011)

Melvyn Bragg, *Rich: The Life of Richard Burton* (1988)

F.G. Cowley, *The Monastic Order in South Wales 1066–1349* (Cardiff,1977)

Matthew Cragoe and Chris Williams, *Wales and War: Society, Politics and Religion in the Nineteenth and Twentieth Centuries* (2007)

John Cule (ed.), *Wales and Medicine* (1975)

John Davies, *A History of Wales* (revised edition, Penguin 2007)

R. R. Davies, 'The Identity of "Wales" in the Thirteenth Century', in R. R. Davies and Geraint H. Jenkins (eds), *From Medieval to Modern Wales: Historical Essays in Honour of Kenneth O. Morgan and Ralph A. Griffiths* (2004)

Russell Davies, *Hope and Heartbreak: A Social History of Wales and the Welsh people, 1776-1871* (2005)

Russell Deacon, *The Welsh Liberals: The History of the Welsh Liberal and Liberal Democrat Parties* (2011)

A.H. Dodd, *The Industrial Revolution in North Wales* (1933)

Chris Evans, *Slave Wales: The Welsh and Atlantic Slavery 1660-1850* (2010)

Madeleine Gray, *Images of Piety* (2000)

Ray Howell, *Searching for the Silures: An Iron Age Tribe in South-East Wales (2009)*

Geraint H. Jenkins, *A Concise History of Wales* (2007)

Philip Jenkins, *A History of Modern Wales, 1536-1990* (1992)

Martin Johnes, *Wales since 1939* (2011)

Gareth Elwyn Jones and Dai Smith, *The People of Wales* (Gomer 1999)

William D. Jones, *Wales in America: Scranton and the Welsh, 1860-1920* (1993)

Frances Lynch, Stephen Aldhouse-Green and Jeffrey L. Davies, *Prehistoric Wales* (2000)

Norbert Ohler, *The Medieval Traveller,* trans. Caroline Hillier (1989)

Katharine K. Olson, *'Ar ffordd Pedr a Phawl:* Welsh Pilgrimage and Travel to Rome, c1200-1530,' *The Welsh History Review* 24 (2008)

J. Beverley Smith, *Llywelyn ap Gruffudd, Prince of Wales* (1998)

Geoffrey Pearson, *Hooligan: A History of Respectable Fears* (1983)

Charlie Whitham, 'Bargaining over Brawdy: Negotiating the American Military Presence in Wales, 1971' in Luis Nunos Rodriguez and Sergiy Glebov (ed), *Military Bases: Historical Perspectives, Contemporary Challenges*, (2009)

Alun Withey, *Physick and the Family: Health Medicine and Care in Wales, 1600–1750* (Manchester, 2011)

Chris Williams and Sian Rhiannon Williams (eds), *Gwent County History*, Volume IV: *Industrial Monmouthshire, 1780-1914* (2011)

Glanmor Williams, *Wales and the Reformation* (Cardiff, 1997)

Glanmor Williams, *The Welsh Church from Conquest to Reformation* (1976)

Picture Acknowledgements

The contributors and publishers gratefully acknowledge the following sources of images:

Western Mail/Media Wales: 25, 26, 36, 42, 45, 52, 56, 57, 69, 76, 80, 85, 94, 100, 106, 114, 122, 128, 131, 134, 136, 138, 141, 143, 146, 147, 151, 153, 155, 157, 162, 164, 167, 168, 170, 174, 176, 179, 180, 183, 186, 189, 191, 193, 194; Dyfed Elis-Gruffydd: 13; Castell Henllys: 16; Anthony Griffiths: 18, 30; Jeremy Moore: 20, 23; The County Council of the City and County of Cardiff: 28; Crown copyright (2011) Visit Wales: 34; Jim Saunders: 39; Hugh Olliff: 41, 47, 51; Jeffrey L. Thomas (www.castlewales. com); Ray Edgar: 63; Keith Bowen: 67; Ken Day: 52, 118; Matthew Rhys: 86–87; South Wales Argus: 89; Huw Evans Agency: 96; David Williams: 99, 102; National Library Wales: 107; J. Elwyn Hughes: 111; Graham Rankin: 117; Thomas Bevan Evans: 123; Bob Taylor: 127.